# THE BODY
# BEAUTIFUL

# THE BODY
# BEAUTIFUL
## Your Guide to Diet, Health and Fitness

### Arline Usden

CHARTWELL
BOOKS, INC.

Published by Chartwell Books, Inc.
A division of Book Sales, Inc.
110 Enterprise Avenue
Secaucus, New Jersey 07094
By arrangement with
Artus Publishing Company Ltd
91 Clapham High Street
London SW4 7TA

ISBN 0–89009–815–8

Design and art direction
by Julia Illingworth
Photography by Ken Martin
Illustrations by Ian Beck

Filmset by Keyspools Ltd
Golborne, Lancs.
Color separations by Newsele
Litho Ltd
Printed in Italy

# CONTENTS

The current fitness boom is more than just a fashion, it has a lot to do with preventive medicine. The idea of healthy, nutritious food and increased exercise is in line with medical recommendations that are designed to make us *less* likely to get disease and *more* likely to live longer.

Keeping yourself in top condition is important for everyone. It is not vanity but essential if you want to make the most of your life. There's no doubt that when you look better, you feel better, too. Get into better shape, whatever your age, and with the extra health and energy, you acquire a feeling of freedom, self-confidence, and vitality – all investments for the future.

We know now that slimming

# INTRODUCTION

has a better chance of being successful when you combine a sensible, healthy reducing plan with increased activity from sport or exercise; that a better body can be acquired with physical effort; and that the infirmities of later years have a lot to do with inactivity. Even the stresses and mental strains of modern living can be reduced once you start to be active rather than passive.

Body maintenance keeps you in good working order, increases the strength and endurance of your muscles, and helps you to gain flexibility. Healthy eating doesn't mean taking vitamin pills, but more fiber in the form of wholewheat bread, potatoes, vegetables, and fruit, and less fat from animal and dairy sources.

This new kind of body refit is far removed from the myths and half-truths of the fringe world of powders and potions and extraordinary notions! You don't have to go for "the burn" to be beautiful, nor do you need to run marathons, get drenched with sweat, or suffer pain. Good health doesn't mean sprinkling bran on your food, and you can get yourself in trim by riding a bike, taking a brisk walk, climbing stairs, or digging the garden, as well as by going to exercise classes.

Body improving exercise or sport should be part of your life-style, at least twenty minutes three times a week if you want to see results. But build up to this gradually if you have been very sedentary.

Activity has to be enjoyable and fun if you are to be motivated enough to continue doing it on a regular basis. So discover the pleasure of sport – there must be *one* you can do! Go out running with a friend or join a club. If you do exercises at home, do them to music, it's easier.

Discover delicious new ways of eating healthily. You'll find you *can* get as much pleasure from eating the foods that are good for you as from eating the ones that are not so good, but which have just become a habit.

After all, fitness isn't a religion! You won't get a medal or go to heaven any sooner – actually by living longer and being healthier, you might get there a bit later!

Get yourself into good shape and you will be slimmer, healthier, and happier, and that is reward enough, isn't it?

# A-Z of Slimming, Health and Fitness

## Aerobics

Exercise that improves the health, strength, and efficiency of heart and lungs. Aerobics as a concept goes back to the 1960s. The difference between aerobic activity and other kinds of exercise is that, when you do something aerobically, you sustain movement over a period of time. This can be running, swimming, even disco dancing. You often need to be fit *before* you start, because many aerobic exercises are too rigorous for beginners.

Work up to a form of aerobic exercise intense enough to raise your pulse to 120 beats a minute for about 30 minutes three times a week.

## Bones

As you age, your bones suffer a steady loss of minerals. In women, this accelerates after the menopause. Physical activity and adequate calcium in your diet can help prevent the bone loss and thus reduce the problems of osteoporosis (brittle bones), fractures, loss of height, and "dowager's hump." Doctors suggest an adequate calcium intake is about 700 mg before the menopause, 1000 mg during it and 1500 mg afterward. Good sources of calcium in food are sardines, muesli, fresh skimmed milk, cheese, cottage cheese, natural yogurt, flour and baking powder.

The water in many areas contains appreciable amounts and cooking foods in hard water can enhance their calcium content. If you cannot get enough from your food, you might require calcium supplements, but ask your doctor first. Eat wholewheat bread and cereals rather than sprinkling bran on foods, because this can interfere with calcium (and iron) absorption.

## Circuit Training

This is a system of continuous weight exercises done at "stations" set up around a course. Each is designed to exercise a different group of muscles and strengthen the heart and lungs. As you get stronger, you can gradually increase the number and strenuousness of the exercises.

## Diets

Slimming diets aim to reduce the amount of calories you eat, so you burn more energy than you take in, and therefore use more of your fat reserves. In the first week of a diet, water loss represents at least 70 percent of the weight loss. Low carbohydrate diets which reduce bread and potatoes lead to most water loss and leave you feeling tired and dehydrated. High protein diets are also not recommended. Your body converts excess protein into ammonia and organic acids and eliminates them through the urine, making your kidneys work overtime. Once you stop dieting, your appetite may boomerang so that you eat more. Exercise is important to help preserve and protect your lean body tissue while you are dieting. If you lose weight without exercise, about 25 to 50 percent of the weight lost will be lean tissue, whatever diet you use.

## Energy

Food provides your body with energy. This is measured in calories. Take in more calories than your body can utilize and it will be stored as fat. If you take in fewer calories than you need, your body will call on its fat deposits – eventually.

## Fat

A woman's natural stores of fat enable her to survive longer without food or even heat. When she becomes too thin, and her fat percentage of body weight falls too low, menstruation ceases and she will be infertile. But too much fat leads to poor health.

Weight alone does not indicate whether you are too fat. Doctors use an implement called skinfold calipers to do an accurate "pinch test" and determine the fat content of your body. The ideal body fat percentage is 25 percent for a woman and 15 percent for a man. But people who exercise regularly have an ideal body fat percentage of 5 percent less. If you are 35 percent fat, you are moderately obese. More than 60 percent fat is gross obesity.

## Glucose

All the carbohydrates you eat are turned to glucose, and pass through the liver to be circulated in the bloodstream. The glucose is used immediately or stored. But the liver can only store up to about 12 hours worth of glucose. That's why breakfast is important — to stop morning fatigue and increase your blood sugar levels. Your brain needs glucose all the time, so depriving yourself of carbohydrates or fasting will make you tired and dizzy.

## Hunger

Eating brings higher levels of glucose in the blood which prompts the release of insulin, but it seems to take about 20 minutes from when you begin eating for your brain to register a feeling of fullness. Insulin enters the bloodstream of a fat person slowly, and this could be one reason why some overweight people eat more and for longer than the slim. This link between insulin and a feeling of fullness is one reason you should not eat quickly if you are slimming. Drinking something like unsweetened grapefruit juice, coffee, or tea *before* a meal also has a "turning down" effect on hunger, as does regular strenuous exercise.

## Isometrics

Exercises that contract muscles and help to strengthen them, without producing movement. There was a lot of interest in this in the 1960s, but it has lost favor today. It has no training effect on heart and lungs, and should not be attempted by anybody with high blood pressure.

## Junk Food

This term is applied, often misleadingly, to a variety of foods.

It is true that some fast foods are high in fat and sugar, and processed foods may include various additives.

However, convenience eating is here to stay, so it pays to read the labels, and to think twice about fast foods when you are slimming.

## Keeping Slim

Once you have got to the weight you want, the problem is how to stay there. If you embark on a fad diet, and do not exercise or change your habits, then the fat will creep back. To keep slim and fit, you need to be more physically active. Once you stop being sedentary, you will be able to eat nutritious food and not think about the calories so much.

## Low Fat

Fat contains twice as many calories as carbohydrates, and too much fat is believed to be bad for your health. So a lower-fat way of eating is sensible. A simple way to cut down is to choose less fatty cuts of meat: poultry and fish rather than red meats and pork. Cut off visible fat and the skin off chicken *after* cooking. Eat fewer sausages, salami, and pies. Eat less hard cheese, butter, and ordinary margarine. Don't fry foods and cut down on cakes, cookies, pastry, and chocolate.

# Metabolism

Metabolism is the sum of all the chemical reactions that happen as your body makes new tissue, produces energy, digests food, and keeps on functioning. Metabolic rates vary. If you are fat, your metabolism may be low, using food for fuel sparingly and storing the rest. Experts now believe that activity is the way to ginger up a sluggish metabolism. Vigorous exercise is thought to encourage the body to use more calories of energy even when the body is at rest.

# Nibbling

It is believed that eating little and often burns off more calories than eating fewer, larger meals. Eating, like exercise, encourages the body's brown fat to burn calories as energy. But, in order to slim down, you must choose your food carefully. Eat fruit and vegetables rather than sugary or fatty foods, chips, cookies, or chocolate. Smaller, more frequent meals also keep insulin levels steady; you are less likely to feel hungry and go on a binge.

# Obesity

Obesity has been defined as an excessive enlargement of the body's total quantity of fat. According to the weight charts, you are obese if you are 20 per cent or more above the "acceptable" weight range.

# Pulse

This is your heart rate, checked by lightly pressing your finger or fingers (not your thumb) on the inside of your wrist, about an inch from the thumb. At rest, an average pulse rate is about 70 to 80 per minute. Taking your own pulse is a guide to how exercise is affecting your body. For your own guideline, subtract your age from 200, then subtract another 40 for unfitness, if you are a beginner. That is the initial maximum rate you should aim for during exercise.

# Quick Weight Loss

Crash dieting is not to be recommended. It took time to get fat and it will take time to get into the habit of better eating and taking more exercise in order to become slim.

# Running

Running is a good way to get fit and lose weight. But you need to start off slowly if you are a novice. Start by taking brisk walks, then walk and run a little. Gradually increase the time you run. Buy a good pair of cushioned running shoes to protect your feet and legs from jarring.

# Smoking

The dangerous effects of cigarette smoking are well documented; they range from heart disease and lung cancer to bronchitis and emphysema. Think of every cigarette smoked as decreasing your life expectancy by about 5 minutes. It is actually less dangerous to be obese than to smoke. But to be both fat and a smoker is to court disaster.

# Thin

Thin people are thought to eat when their bodies tell them they are hungry, while fat people may eat in response to cues from their surroundings. However, being thin is also a matter of genetic inheritance.

# Unsaturated Fats

The sort that stay liquid at room temperature such as sunflower or maize oil, or margarines called "polyunsaturated" are thought by many experts to be better than the animal fats found in eggs, meat, hard cheese, whole milk, butter, and ordinary margarine. But try to reduce *all* fats in your diet.

# Vitamins

These are simply trace elements in food which are vital to health. A diet which includes fresh fruit and vegetables, as well as wholewheat cereals or bread, should provide all the vitamins you need. Smoking reduces Vitamin C uptake, and you may need to take extra food or vitamin supplements if you are old or ill, or have tooth problems that stop you eating a varied diet. But vitamin pills are not an insurance policy and you should never take any pill as a matter of course.

# Water

The body has a big percentage of water, and it is useless to try and restrict your liquid intake in order to lose weight. The body adjusts its water levels, and any water lost at a sauna or through heat is soon replaced.

# Xtreme

It is not a good idea to go on extreme diets of any kind. Crash dieting is pointless in terms of weight loss that stays off.

# YoYo Syndrome

This is the disappointing lose-weight-regain-weight fact of life for many dieters, who try to slim by reducing food intake alone. Any diet that reduces the calories you eat will cause a weight loss, whether it is healthy or not. But, unless you exercise, you will lose lean tissue. A very stringent diet educates your body into thinking it is in a state of famine—so it tries to store food (in the form of fat). Too many diets can actually lower your metabolism.

The weight lost fastest is weight regained fastest. As soon as you stop dieting, you regain the lost weight, but as fat rather than the muscle you have lost. So you may actually be fatter than before. Exercise helps preserve and protect your lean body tissue while you are dieting.

To lose weight permanently, you need to lose weight *slowly* on a nutritious well-planned diet (1200 to 1500 calories a day, preferably) together with a program of exercise. The key to weight control is also a change of life-style, to alter the behavior that made you fat in the first place.

Fat people do not necessarily overeat. In fact, thin active people generally eat *more* than fat sedentary people. The obese may have faulty body mechanisms governing their output of energy and storage of fat, but they can be altered with time.

# Zen Macrobiotic Diet

A quasi-mystical fad diet, it can lead to mineral imbalance, vitamin deficiencies and rapid loss of lean tissue rather than fat.

# DOES YOUR BODY NEED A REFIT?

**Bad health may be just a matter of bad luck, but doctors now believe that unhealthy living plays a part. Is your life-style contributing to present or future ailments? You *can* lower the risks of preventable illness and it is never too late to begin. It is possible to increase your life expectancy and to make it more enjoyable by becoming fit and vigorous enough to be as active as you would wish. You cannot remove all the risks but you can modify your habits – i.e. eat less fat and exercise more regularly. We often deceive ourselves about the true state of our bodies and our feelings, so try this questionnaire to evaluate your physical and mental well-being – and be truthful! Then remember that your life is to a large extent in your own hands.**

## Smoking

This powerful and easily acquired addiction is certainly one of the most destructive anti-health habits of all. The recruitment of young smokers continues, and, with girls, may even be increasing. This is what smoking can lead to. . . .

### Heart Disease

Carbon monoxide in cigarettes reduces the capacity of the blood to carry oxygen and also contributes to preventing the blood releasing oxygen to the heart. Nicotine in cigarettes acts like an injection of adrenaline, pushing up pulse rate and blood pressure, so that the heart actually needs more oxygen. One cigarette can increase the heartbeat from about 77 beats a minute to 88 beats a minute and your blood pressure rises. It will make no difference if you smoke low-tar cigarettes. But give up smoking and the risks disappear within five years.

The carbon monoxide also seems to encourage the accumulation of fatty deposits in the arteries. Smokers are twice as likely to have heart problems as nonsmokers and up to five times as likely in the 35 to 44 age group.

### Cancer

Compared to nonsmokers, the average smoker (15 to 20 cigarettes a day) is 14 times more likely to die from cancer of the mouth, throat, and lung, and four times more likely to get cancer of the bladder. It is the tar in cigarette smoke that is considered to be carcinogenic. Cancer of the bladder can result from carcinogenic substances being absorbed into the bloodstream and being excreted in urine.

Lung cancer is nearly *always* caused by smoking. Only about three in 1,000 cases occur in lifelong nonsmokers. More than half those with lung cancer had bronchitis first. Bronchial carcinoma is the most common form of cancer in the Western world. Your chances of getting the disease depend on how many cigarettes you smoke a day. If you are a light smoker, you are ten times as likely to get the disease as nonsmokers. If you are a heavy smoker, you are 25 times more susceptible.

### Bronchitis

Smoking causes chronic bronchitis.

Even the children of heavy smokers may get bronchitis from breathing in smoke-filled rooms. Inhaled smoke is an irritant that damages air sacs and the bronchial passages and tubes, causing chronic breathlessness and disability.

## Other Problems

Smoking also reduces the blood supply to the womb in pregnant women, and babies of women smokers are on average 7 oz (200 g) lighter than those of nonsmokers. A pregnant woman who smokes 15 to 20 cigarettes a day is twice as likely to have a miscarriage or a premature baby as a nonsmoker.

Two out of five smokers on 20 or more cigarettes a day die before the age of 65.

Think of every cigarette smoked as decreasing your life expectancy by about 5 minutes.

# Cholesterol

This is a steroid chemical, naturally present in the body, and also found in such foods as fatty meat, eggs, and dairy products. High blood concentrations of cholesterol denote an increased risk of coronary heart disease caused by the narrowing of the arteries by deposits of fat. A low-fat, low-cholesterol diet can lower the risk of heart disease, doctors claim, and, as a result of recent research – a ten-year American study which showed conclusively that high-risk patients can reduce the likelihood of heart attacks with the aid of diet and drugs – a case has been made for cholesterol reduction in the population as a whole.

Cholesterol is transported between organs and tissues of the body by the blood lipoproteins – and there are "good" and "bad" varieties. Low-density lipoproteins, known as LDL, *deposit* the fatty substance in cells, while the high density sort (HDL) have been shown to remove it, *reducing* fat and cholesterol in your arteries.

So it is a good idea to raise your HDL levels. What helps? Eating more fish is one suggestion. (It's the fish oils that may help to reduce the risk of heart attack.) Taking more exercise is another. Several studies have demonstrated that an exercise program based on jogging can lead to higher HDL levels. The threshold

# HOW HEALTHY ARE YOU?

This quiz tests your general health, mental health, stress or lack of it.

| | YES | NO |
|---|---|---|
| 1 Are you within the recommended weight limits for your height? (See page 23.) | +6 pts | −6 pts |
| 2 Can you walk up three flights of stairs (of about 15 steps each flight) without pausing to catch your breath? | +5 pts | −5 pts |
| 3 Are you a nonsmoker? | +6 pts | −6 pts |
| 4 Have you been a nonsmoker for 15 years or more? | +6 pts | −6 pts |
| 5 Do you rarely take patent medicines? | +3 pts | −3 pts |
| 6 Do you usually sleep well? | +4 pts | −4 pts |
| 7 Are you happy with your work? | +5 pts | −5 pts |
| 8 Do you drive less than 20,000 miles a year? | +3 pts | −3 pts |
| 9 Do you eat fresh fruit and vegetables every day? | +4 pts | −4 pts |
| 10 Do you drink (on average) 3 to 4 cans (1 liter) of beer or less per day? Or 4 glasses of wine or less? Or 2 jiggers of spirits or less? | +4 pts | −4 pts |
| 11 Do you exercise three times a week (or more)? | +6 pts | −6 pts |
| 12 Are you good natured and calm most of the time, rarely tense, nervous, or irritable? | +4 pts | −4 pts |
| 13 Have you got a pleasant, satisfying, well-balanced family life? | +3 pts | −3 pts |
| 14 Do you eat a healthy diet, low in fat and sugar but with plenty of fruit, vegetables, whole cereals, and have you cut down on sweets, cookies, cakes, fried food, and fatty meat? | +6 pts | −6 pts |
| 15 Do you have regular cervical smear checkups and examine your own breasts? | +4 pts | −4 pts |
| 16 Are you (as far as you know) free of ailments of any kind, including asthma, diabetes, arthritis? | +6 pts | −6 pts |
| 17 Do you have dental checkups at least every six months? | +3 pts | −3 pts |
| 18 Is your mother alive and well? Or did she live beyond 73 years? | +3 pts | −3 pts |
| 19 Is your father alive and well? Or did he live beyond 68? | +3 pts | −3 pts |
| 20 Do you find it easy to get along with other people? | +2 pts | −2 pts |
| 21 Do you bother about your appearance? | +2 pts | −2 pts |
| 22 Do you have interests and hobbies apart from your work and home? | +2 pts | −2 pts |
| 23 Do you feel in control of yourself and your life? | +2 pts | −2 pts |
| 24 Have you *not* had any major upheaval or bereavement for some time? | +4 pts | −4 pts |
| 25 Are you without substantial debts or mortgage repayments that you find hard to cope with? | +4 pts | −4 pts |
| 26 Have you *not* had jet lag twice or more in the past year? | +4 pts | −4 pts |
| 27 Have you *not* been admitted to hospital for illness or injury in the last five years? | +5 pts | −5 pts |
| 28 Do you feel you have enough energy to enjoy a social life after work? | +2 pts | −2 pts |
| 29 Are you free of allergies? | +2 pts | −2 pts |
| 30 Do you have a regular and happy relationship that has lasted for some time? | +3 pts | −3 pts |

**YOUR SCORE  There is a total of 116 points for Yes answers. The lower your score, the less rosy the picture for your health and well-being.**
**100 points and over: BRILLIANT** You must be healthy.
**50 to 99 points: VERY GOOD** You really do seem to have been very lucky and to have terrific motivation and self-control. Nothing much to worry about here. But check that you have enough exercise in your life.
**0 to 49 points: GOOD** There are questions in the quiz that are not personally controllable. You could well be leading a healthy life and lose points on things you cannot do anything about. This is a good score – but don't get complacent.
**−50 to 0 points: FAIR** You still have quite a way to go. It is important to build in time for leisure and hobbies and find ways of countering stress.
**−116 to −49 points: POOR** You can't be all that healthy with a score like this. Quite a lot seems to be wrong. Should you be rethinking your life-style altogether? The main ways to improve your health are (a) stop smoking, (b) eat a healthier diet and (c) take up regular exercise. **Note** You can never be really healthy if you smoke.

running distance is about eight miles a week, which is thought to be attainable by many people.

Stress also plays a part because in some people stress hormones change the body chemistry so that the blood becomes loaded with cholesterol. So learning how to relax can be as important as reducing your fat intake.

According to heart research doctors, the cholesterol response to stress is a hallmark of some "Type A" personalities. These coronary-prone, hard-driving, high-achievers are impatient, quick to anger, hostile and aggressive, and have total job involvement. "Type B" personalities are calmer and more laid back.

Exercise may help here, too, because studies show that regular exercisers make less adrenaline under stress than inactive people. This is one of the hormones mobilized by stress that release fat into the blood.

## Diet and cancer prevention

The American Government has taken the unprecedented step of endorsing an anti-cancer diet. Cigarettes, too much wine, thick juicy steaks, fish-and-chips, and prolonged sunbathing are all on the forbidden list. They advise:
● Eat less food high in both saturated and unsaturated fat, particularly fatty cuts of meat, whole-milk dairy products, cooking oils and fats.
● Eat more fruit, vegetables, and wholegrain cereal products daily, especially those high in Vitamin C and sources of Vitamin A (the carotene in red-colored vegetables, which converts to Vitamin A in the body).
● Cut down on all salt-cured, salt-pickled, and smoked foods such as smoked sausage, smoked fish, and bacon.
● Drink alcohol only in moderation.

Fiber in the diet protects against cancer of the colon, but the type of fiber is important, according to the Dunn Nutrition Unit in Cambridge. The protection factors against colonic cancer in the high-fiber diet are the pentose sugars. Different fiber foods contain different amounts of pentose. Soya and wheat products are good sources. Broccoli, sprouts, and cabbage also contain significant amounts. Pears and plums have moderate amounts and rice and oats very little. Foods with a high pentose content increase stool weight and this may in turn protect against bowel cancer by diluting possible carcinogens.

## Alcohol

Drinking is a social pleasure and alcohol only becomes a risk when it is taken to excess. Dependence on alcohol can ruin a marriage, interfere with work, and lead to chronic ill health, but the barrier between a regular social drinker and the problem drinker can be a narrow one. It is as well to learn to recognize the danger signals while you can.

Do you turn to drink for consolation? Do you have bouts of bad memory after drinking? Do you *need* to have quite a lot to drink every day? (See page 11.) Do you find yourself unable to stop drinking once you start? Then it looks as though you may well have crossed that barrier and need expert help.

Alcohol is a drug and like any drug it becomes harmful if taken too regularly and in excessive amounts. For slimmers, it is also as well to remember that alcohol is full of calories, but of little nutritional value.

The effects of alcohol are cumulative and it takes several hours for it to be eliminated from the body, which should always be remembered by car drivers. Eating food, even titbits, helps to slow down the rate of alcohol absorption, and the slower you take your drink the less effect.

## Stress

The strains of life affect you both mentally and physically. Stress symptoms can include headaches, heartburn, memory lapses, asthma, backache, and an irritable colon. Stress-related diseases include diseases of the digestive tract such as ulcers and colitis, attacks of angina, and even alopecia areata – a type of baldness.

Are you under too much stress? How can you tell? Exhaustion caused by physical activity is normal and good for you, but exhaustion caused by rage and despair is bad. The most common causes of stress are being unable to understand or change or control what is happening to you – you feel helpless and at the mercy of others.

This table of Life Change Units will help you to work out your own stress factor. The higher your total, the more likely you are to suffer from illness, so make some positive efforts. Tick any life changes that have happened to you *during the past year*, then add up your total points.

### TEST YOUR STRESS

| Events | Units |
|---|---|
| Death of husband or wife | 100 |
| Marital separation | 65 |
| Death of a close family member | 63 |
| Personal injury or illness | 53 |
| Marriage | 50 |
| Loss of job | 47 |
| Marital reconciliation | 45 |
| Retirement | 45 |
| Change in health of a member of the family | 44 |
| Pregnancy | 40 |
| Sex difficulties | 39 |
| Gaining a new member of the family | 39 |
| Change in financial status | 38 |
| Death of a close friend | 37 |
| Change to a different kind of work | 36 |
| Increase or decrease of arguments with wife or husband | 35 |
| Taking out a large home mortgage | 31 |
| Foreclosure of mortgage or loan | 30 |
| Change in work responsibilities | 29 |
| Son or daughter leaving home | 29 |
| Trouble with your in-laws | 29 |
| Outstanding personal achievement | 28 |
| Beginning or stopping work | 26 |
| Revision of personal habits | 24 |
| Trouble with a business superior | 23 |
| Change of work hours or conditions | 20 |
| Change of house | 20 |
| Change of school | 20 |
| Change in recreation | 19 |
| Change in social activities | 18 |

*Results:* *Comparison of a group of 5000 individuals showed that there was a high correlation between their life change scores and their subsequent medical history.*
*Over 300: You are in a group likely to suffer illness.*
*200–299: You are moderately at risk.*
*150–199: You have a minor chance of becoming ill in the next year.*
*Below that, you should be able to cope without your health being affected.*

## How to relieve tension

**1** Don't try to be perfect at everything. If you work full-time, you will need help in the house.
**2** Plan escape periods, when you can be alone.
**3** Put your house in order. Physically tidying up chaos can help your mind, too.
**4** Don't procrastinate. Organize your time realistically so that you do not have to complete something in a tearing, frantic hurry.
**5** Make yourself a list of attainable objectives (e.g. decide to walk halfway home each day), then tick each one off as you complete it. Small successes build confidence.
**6** Have you enough leisure in your life? You can pursue success so recklessly that the spiritual and personal side of your life may be neglected.
**7** Set your priorities. Don't devote as much time to trivia as you do to the important things of life. It is more important to talk to your children and play with them than to dust the whole house every day.
**8** Try listening to others without interrupting.
**9** Take a break. Holidays are an extremely important way of cutting off from the normal stresses and strains of both home and job.
**10** Try to avoid aggression. Turn to humor rather than argument.
**11** Learn to say no. In the end, please yourself.
**12** Investigate meditation, yoga, autogenic training – therapies that help you to cope with stress.

# Top to Toe Guide to Body Maintenance

## HAIR: Give it a super service

As you have up to 200,000 hairs on your head, losing about fifty or more a day isn't a problem. Your hair is continually replacing itself, with the life of a single hair being three to five years. Hair grows about half an inch a month and hormones affect its growth and appearance.

Keeping the hair and scalp healthy begins with shampooing — wash as often as your hair needs it. Although based on detergent, modern shampoos are often gentle, and formulated not to wash out *all* of the hair's natural oils, which keep it manageable.

Use one application of shampoo if hair is over-oily, shampoo frequently but use warm, not hot, water and do not stimulate the scalp by massaging.

Use a conditioner to make your hair easier to comb through. By adhering to the outer hair scales, and making hair less fly-away and tangly, conditioners have a purely cosmetic effect. Think of cherishing your hair, rather than nourishing it. You cannot "feed" hair (it is dead when it leaves the scalp), but conditioners carry cationic ingredients to neutralize static electricity; polymers (plastics) to give body; protein to help repair damage; and oils to add luster and reduce friction by smoothing the outer scales.

Protein in "deep action" conditioners repairs damaged hair by forming a sheath around thin or broken hair fibers, making them stronger. But you are only helping the *visible* condition.

Comb through conditioners with a wide-toothed comb or widely spaced plastic styling brush. Don't use a normal bristle brush on wet hair because this is when it is at its weakest and you could cause splits and breakage. Start combing through tangles from the

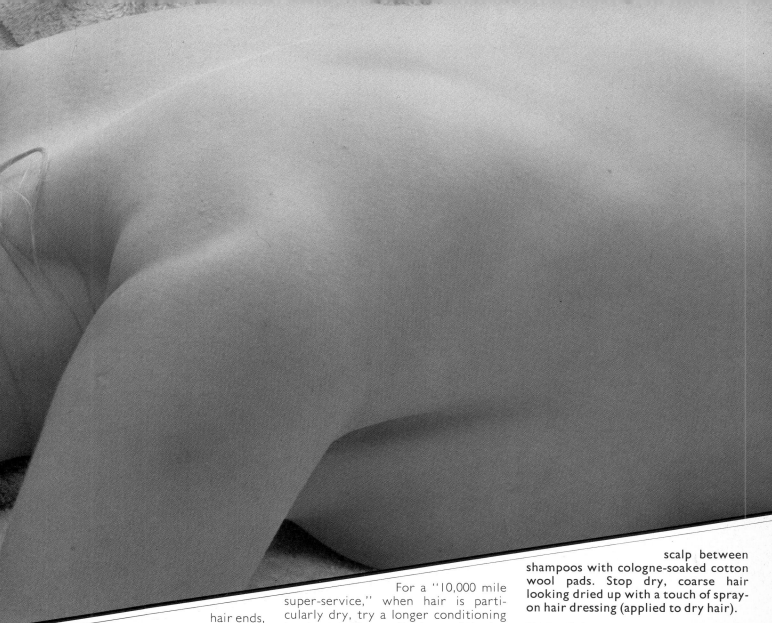

hair ends, gradually working up to the scalp.

Most of the processes we inflict on our hair to improve its color, texture, or style are damaging. The idea is to use modern hair products to get the effect you want with the *least* damage.

Bleaches, permanent colorants and perms need to penetrate the hair's outer scales into the cortex beneath to work and so affect porosity. Once the outer scales are forced open chemically, they are hard to close and the hair becomes "processed" looking. Heated rollers, stylers, and dryers are likely to cause dryness and breakage from heat damage. Nature, too, can be an enemy to your hair's beauty because hot sunlight strips away natural oil and acts like a bleach on color.

For normal servicing, use a simple rinse-out conditioner every time you wash your hair if it is normal-to-dry. If it is oily, apply conditioner (if at all) to dry porous ends only.

For a "10,000 mile super-service," when hair is particularly dry, try a longer conditioning treatment. Use a suitable conditioning cream or hair wax, or a cup of warm oil such as olive, almond or castor (stand the cup in hot water to heat). Leave on for about an hour. Hot towels or a plastic cap help to keep in the warmth, encouraging the conditioning ingredients to stick. Afterward, rinse out conditioner or shampoo oil out of your hair.

**RUNNING REPAIRS** Dandruff is an exaggeration of the scaling process by which skin normally renews itself and has been attributed to many causes. There's no actual cure but you can control the problem. For most ordinary "snowstorm" dandruff flaking, try a shampoo containing the ingredient zinc pyrithione. If the dandruff is red and itchy see your doctor.

Swab down an oily

scalp between shampoos with cologne-soaked cotton wool pads. Stop dry, coarse hair looking dried up with a touch of spray-on hair dressing (applied to dry hair).

# FACE: How to get longer mileage

The skin of your face, like that of your hands, is constantly exposed to sunlight and the elements and therefore tends to weather and age more quickly than the skin on the covered-up parts of the body. Protection is vital in order to stave off premature wrinkles. This means using a sunfilter cream every time you sunbathe, even if you tan easily, because ultra violet A and B light attack the skin's inner collagen and elastic tissue.

**Cleansing.** If you use make-up, cleansing cream, or lotion removers are effective for taking

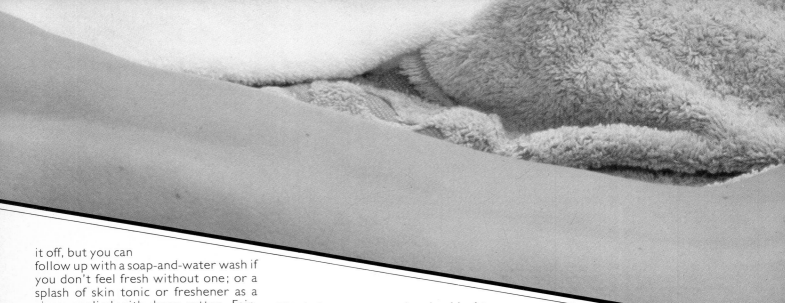

it off, but you can follow up with a soap-and-water wash if you don't feel fresh without one; or a splash of skin tonic or freshener as a rinse, applied with damp cotton. Fair, sensitive skins sometimes react to the alkaline and drying effects of normal soap and are better with mild cleansing creams or lotions that do not contain perfume. If your skin is oily, soap-and-water cleansing is excellent. But rinse very thoroughly.

**Moisturizing** creams contain oil to help supplement the skin's natural oil barrier. This holds in the skin's moisture, which tends to be reduced by washing and weather. For the best effect apply moisturizer to the face when the skin is still slightly damp. Don't forget to treat your neck too.

The most beautiful complexions are those of children whose grease glands are small, turned down to the lowest setting. At the onset of puberty, testosterone, the male hormone (produced more or less by both sexes), switches on the grease glands to full production – higher in teenage boys than girls. Alas, with the increase in the skin's grease, come the problems of blackheads, whiteheads, and pimples, and the fine, delicate, even-pored skin of the child gives way to the often angry, blemished and coarser-pored skin of the adolescent.

Few escape the consequences, but your type of skin has a lot to do with your genetic inheritance. Women also find that pimples, and greasy skin and hair seem to get worse just before a period, probably because of changing hormone levels.

**RUNNING REPAIRS** Use a pimple preparation that contains benzoyl peroxide to help dry up pimples and encourage peeling.

This helps to remove the plug blocking the grease gland, which is the cause of the problem. If you are sensitive to the ingredient and get a rash, try products containing sulfur and resorcinol.

If your skin looks muddy and flaky, try a home peeling or exfoliating treatment. Gently scrub the face with a complexion brush or rough wash cloth, or mix up a little oatmeal to a paste and rub the grainy mixture into the skin (avoiding your eyes) with little circular movements, then rinse off.

# SKIN: Polish up your chassis

Good hygiene is the key to a healthy, good-looking skin and helps the body's largest organ to keep in good running order. Composed of several layers, with the bottom, basal layer of cells continuously dividing, the skin is constantly renewing itself. It takes about twenty-eight days for a cell to rise to the surface and flake off. Dirt, waste products from the body, oil and bacteria cover the surface, so it is necessary to wash every day in order to remove them. Not that you can remove all the bacteria, of course, nor would you wish to. They are part of the body's natural ecological environment and most are completely harmless. Although flaking-off cells take dirt and some debris with them, if you don't wash it is possible for fungi, dirt and bacteria to become trapped and cause problems, not the least of them being body odor.

An all-over soap-and-water wash and a change of underclothes, socks, or panty hose daily is the first line of defense against

perspiration smell; while anti-perspirants, containing aluminum salts (which have an astringent effect on sweat glands, reducing sweat production to a certain extent), and deodorants (containing bactericides to reduce the number of bacteria on the skin surface) are the important back-up. Perspiration itself is odorless, but the apocrine glands, sited in the armpits and genital areas, produce a fluid that contains salts and nitrogenous and fatty compounds, and these are attacked by bacteria, causing odor.

At bathtime, friction mitts and straps can be used to give a stimulating scrub that removes dead cells and gingers up the circulation, especially useful on the backs of the arms where you can get goosepimply skin, or between the shoulders.

**RUNNING REPAIRS** Remove underarm hair, because moist, poorly ventilated places are a breeding ground for the bacteria that lead to body odor. But do not apply an anti-perspirant deodorant straight after shaving in case of irritation and soreness.

Smooth dry skin and prolong a tan by using oil in the bath instead of salts or bubbles, and rub in a body lotion all over every time you bathe. Legs have fewer oil glands and are especially prone to dryness.

# HANDS: Keep them in working order

Nails are made from the same kind of keratin protein as the outer layer of skin but it is packed together far more densely. The growing part is under the lunula or half moon at the base of the nail, and the nail actually originates nearly as far back

as the last finger joint.

Nail growth slows down in colder weather and speeds up in warm summers. (Toenails grow at half the rate of fingernails.) Ridges and imperfections in the nail can be attributed to illness or injury.

Household detergents do most damage to hands and nails because they remove grease. Wear rubber gloves (but not for more than 15 to 20 minutes at a time), or better still, wear thin cotton gloves inside to prevent your hands sweating.

**RUNNING REPAIRS** Use hand lotion every time you have your hands in water. Use a pencil to dial telephone numbers to help prevent nails breaking. Nail polish can act as a shield to fragile nails, but polish remover is drastically degreasing. So touch up nails rather than removing polish too frequently.

When giving yourself a manicure, don't ever poke at your cuticles with sharp metal instruments.

# BACK: Look after your danger zone

Back pain is one of the most common ailments, with a great many causes, and results in a lot of distress and many days lost from work. Bad lifting and posture are often to blame and, if you wear very high heels that give inadequate support and cause ankle wobble, it is your back that takes the strain. An over-soft bed can lead to problems. The flatter you sleep the better, so banish too many pillows and manage with just one.

When you want to pick up a weight (or a child) do not bend over from the waist, but crouch down, bending your knees, hold the weight close to your body and rise slowly, using your thigh muscles for leverage rather than your back. Check your chair at work. Is it giving enough support to your lumbar area? When shopping, do not put all your purchases into one basket. Divide them into two bags and be more evenly balanced.

Weak stomach muscles could contribute to back disorders. Try strengthening them with exercise.

You can lose years, pounds, and inches in a moment, and look after your back, with good posture. It helps to prevent back pain and stresses. Pull in your stomach muscles, tuck your bottom under, keep your shoulders back and down, relaxed but not stiff, and hold your head high as if it were being pulled up from the ceiling.

**RUNNING REPAIRS** Check with your doctor before doing any exercises if you have back pain. But if he gives you the go ahead, see if these help. Lie down on the floor on your back, knees bent, arms at your sides. Tighten your stomach and buttock muscles and tuck in your chin to flatten your neck against the floor. Hold for a count of 5. Relax.

Repeat this exercise, but this time bend one knee, pulling it up to try and touch your nose. Hold for 5 counts, then relax slowly.

A good way to get relief from back pain is to lie on your side on a bed or sofa curled in the fetal position, with knees bent and slightly forward, chin forward on the chest.

# MUSCLES: Don't have a breakdown

Muscle is a machine – a nervous impulse switches it on and chemical reactions provide the energy for contractions. There are over 600 muscles in your body, each made up of bundles of closely connecting muscle fibers. Without exercise they tend to become smaller and weaker or virtually disappear if they are not used.

Exercise produces biochemical changes within the muscles used, which improve their oxygen supply and therefore endurance. If you do regular exercise (training), you can work harder and for longer with less effort.

Muscles lose size and strength as we grow older, but it is disuse rather than aging that is to blame for much of the loss. As you would imagine, your maximum strength is achieved between the ages of twenty to thirty. Thereafter, most muscle groups progressively decline in strength. There is a reduction of 3 to 5 percent in muscle mass for each decade, due to loss of muscle protein from inactivity, aging or both.

Vigorous exercise tends to increase the rate that protein is built up in skeletal muscle, while at the same time retarding its rate of breakdown. An important point, because weight loss by diet alone causes a significant loss of

lean tissue (muscle). Exercise appears to protect against these lean tissue losses, and so more of the weight lost through diet is *fat* loss.

You cannot change muscle to fat nor fat to muscle. (Fat is stored in fat cells under the skin.) If you eat too much and exercise too little, any calories beyond those needed to fuel the body will be stored as fat. However, the more exercise you do, the more you build muscle tissue and help reduce fat. Because with more muscle, you burn more calories.

Spot reduction? Experts say you may be able to tighten up muscles selectively but this will not affect the overlay of fat on a potbelly or flabby bottom if you are overweight. Sit-ups won't make your stomach disappear and rolling around on your rear end will not flatten it out. When you lose fat, by reducing your calorie intake, you lose it from all over the body and you cannot choose one specific area – alas!

Losing weight requires you to burn up more calories than you eat and you burn most calories by using the *most*

muscles, by being active and doing vigorous activities. Therefore, limiting your exercise to just one set of muscles isn't sensible.

**RUNNING REPAIRS** Learn to relax your muscles as an antidote to stress. When you feel strained, you tend to hold your muscles tight without realizing it. To recognize muscle tension, screw up your face and grit your teeth. Now relax and let your jaw sag open. Feel the difference.

At prenatal relaxation classes, mothers-to-be are taught how to relax by tensing and releasing muscles all over the body. It is a technique that works for everyone. Try relaxing in a warm, quiet room. Lie on a bed, in a comfortable armchair or even on the floor, with a pile of cushions. Begin by taking two or three deep breaths. Breathe in slowly and deeply and breathe out slowly. Now clench and release each set of muscles in turn, starting at your feet and working up the calves, thighs, buttocks, stomach, chest, fingers, hands, arms, shoulders, neck and finally your face. The idea is to go absolutely limp. Breathe slowly and deeply and try saying the word "peace" (or anything else you wish) each time you breathe out.

**Note**

Tired muscles and cold muscles are especially liable to tearing and injury, so always do warm-ups first before you start any exercise regime.

# LEGS: Check your bodywork

Diet and exercise will help to slim down your legs, but you will have to plan on a long-term gradual improvement because quick weight loss on crash diets is usually a failure (you lose water, not fat) and firming-up exercises take consistent effort over a period of time to achieve results.

The shape and length of your legs is probably hereditary and it is certainly true that varicose veins seem to run in families.

Troublesome rather than disabling, varicose veins are twisted and swollen and occur when the valves in the veins do not work efficiently. The common early symptom is the appearance of a prominent swollen bluish vein. The leg aches and your foot may become swollen after standing. You are more prone to get varicose veins if you are fat, pregnant, very tall, come from a Celtic background, have fine, thin skin, or if you spend most of your working day standing fairly still and not moving around. If you think you are suscep-

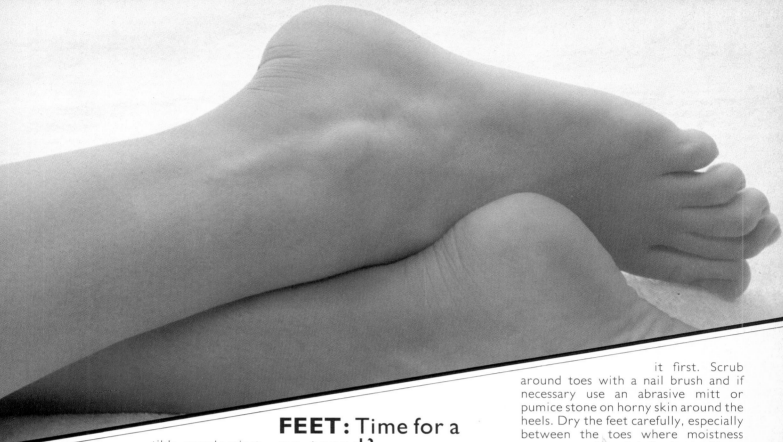

tible, guard against varicose veins by trying to keep off your feet as much as possible – sit with your legs up, raised above chest level. Wear support tights. Varicose veins can be treated by surgery or injections, so consult your doctor.

**RUNNING REPAIRS** The skin on your legs tends to dry out, especially in summer, so keep it lubricated with body lotions or creams. Older skin is less efficient in retaining moisture and soon becomes dry and chapped with too much soap and water – so don't linger too long in the bath, or have a shower instead.

Remove superfluous hair from legs regularly to keep them smooth. Shaving is quickest but as the hair is chopped off at skin level, it grows back quickly and feels bristly. Depilatory creams dissolve hair chemically from just under the skin, but they sometimes cause irritation and the hair soon returns. Waxing is probably the best method for legs because it pulls out hair from the roots (if the technique is right) and the hair takes longer to grow back, sometimes several weeks. Every time a hair is pulled from the root, it has a discouraging effect on it, so regular waxing may result in thinner, weaker regrowth. Hot waxing is best left to beauty salons, but you can try cold waxing kits or strips (less good) at home. It is worth saving up for a leg and "bikini" waxing session at a salon just before a holiday.

## FEET: Time for a re-tread?

The only time most of us think about our feet is when they hurt or are on show in summer sandals. The twenty-six bones in each foot, together with their ligaments and muscles, form a perfect mechanism, yet because of the way we often treat them with badly fitting shoes, most feet are far from beautiful.

Very high heels cause the most problems. They push the foot forward so that toes become cramped. Change your shoes daily (or even twice daily) and leave them to air between wearings.

Try some foot exercises to increase circulation and help stiffness and tiredness. Rotate your ankles. Stand on a thick telephone book and curl your toes over the edge. Sit or lie down with legs straight and try to spread out your toes. Flex and extend your feet. Stand with your feet together and slowly rise on to tiptoes. Raise and lower the heels several times. Walk around barefoot whenever you find a suitable opportunity. After these exercises, massage each toe separately, using a cream or body lotion.

Give your feet a pedicure every week. After a bath is best, when toenails are easier to cut. If you wear nail polish, remove it first. Scrub around toes with a nail brush and if necessary use an abrasive mitt or pumice stone on horny skin around the heels. Dry the feet carefully, especially between the toes where moistness encourages fungal infections. About every three to four weeks cut your toenails straight across to discourage ingrowing and smooth off the edges with an emery board or nail file. Leave nails long enough to cover the tip of the toe. Clean under the nails with an orange stick. Carefully trim off any hang nails, but don't clip or push back the cuticles or you may damage the new nail. Massage in body lotion or foot cream. If you wish to reapply nail polish, swab over each nail first with remover to take away traces of grease.

**RUNNING REPAIRS** Rub callouses, which are areas of dead skin that build up under the sole of the foot (caused by friction and pressure), with an abrasive foot file or foot sponge with an abrasive surface, then smooth on a rich lubricating cream or lotion. Corns are also caused by friction and pressure from shoes, but it is best to avoid home remedies using salicylic acid and see a chiropodist who will remove them quickly and painlessly. If you suffer from sweaty feet, a daily wash and change of panty hose or socks is essential, of course, but you can also try using a refreshing foot deodorant spray during the day. It dries quickly so you can spray it through hose.

# Body Changes Through Life

During our expected three score years and ten we eat about 35 tons (35,525 kg) of food, yet in old age we may well end up very little heavier than we were in our twenties. Food provides energy and builds and renews bone, tissue and muscle, but whether or not you have an obesity problem depends on the balance between calories eaten and calories expended. At each stage of growth and maturity there are pressures and problems.

Our genetic inheritance will influence the shape of our bodies, so tall parents are likely to have a tall child, but at birth babies usually start out about equal when it comes to body fat. It is over-feeding that results in the over-plump baby, no longer considered a bonny picture of health. A breast-fed baby is never likely to over-feed, but concentrated bottle feeds and early weaning on to cereals can result in a fat child. Anxious mothers may mistake crying from thirst as a hunger cry, or feel tempted to give food as a panacea for all ills.

Obesity tends to run in families because of their life-style and eating habits and it takes a great effort by parents to break their customary routines and help a fat child lose weight and become active. An obese boy or girl is inevitably less active than his or her thinner friends and this sedentary behavior tips the scales even though they may not eat more than children who are slim.

Children who are overweight mature earlier – fat girls tend to menstruate early (menstruation does not usually occur until a weight of at least 98 pounds (45 kg) is reached).

"Puppy fat" implies a weight problem that disappears with adulthood, but this is not necessarily the case. Today's children have a less active life-style than previous generations. They go to school by car or bus instead of walking; they watch television rather than taking part in more active pursuits; they have more opportunities for sugary and fatty snacks and nibbles that are high in calories, and probably more money to spend on them.

At adolescence, increased output of female sex hormones causes girls to lay down fat at a faster rate than boys, while the male sex hormone encourages the development of muscles. Most teenage girls start to gain fatty tissue in early teenage years because one of the major functions of the hormone estrogen is to promote the storage of fat in preparation for pregnancy.

Men are lucky to have more muscle tissue since muscle burns calories faster than fat does and as men are usually taller and heavier, with larger bones, they require a lot more calories a day to maintain a steady weight than women do; and they use a higher expenditure of energy for most physical exertion. This means men can lose weight much more quickly than women who are on the same kind of diet and who do the same amount of physical exercise.

We like what we get accustomed to, so if your family has always gone in for fried foods, big portions, baked desserts, and plenty of cookies, cakes, and chocolate, with little enthusiasm for fruit and fresh vegetables, it may need more self-discipline than a child or teenager can muster to change the pattern and lose weight.

As a young adult, the most active time of your life, there is great pressure to become sexually desirable and this is when most overweight girls do their utmost to lose the surplus pounds. The danger is turning to crash diets and the yo-yo syndrome of weight-loss-soon-regained, with the body's metabolism becoming more efficient with every diet – determined to lay down fat, however little you seem to eat, because it is preparing for the famine (diet) it expects tomorrow!

Women's weight fluctuates more than men's because of their changing hormonal levels throughout the menstrual cycle. As the level of progesterone rises in relation to the amount of estrogen just before the menstrual period, women tend to retain water in their tissues – some can gain as much as 5 or 6 pounds

(2.5 kg) in weight at this time.

Also, premenstrually, many women have cravings for sweet and salty foods. This tendency to have cravings seems more pronounced in the overweight. Possibly, as one promising theory suggests, because they have a cravings-causing shortage of progesterone. Other experts suspect a reduction in the supply of the brain chemical serotonin, which acts as a mood-elevator and appetite suppressant.

Getting married puts a much bigger emphasis on food – cooking for two, shopping, giving dinner parties; and social life seems to centre round food and drink. If leisure time is also sedentary, it's all too easy to start getting fatter. Build in more activity, and the balance will be better.

With pregnancy, many women find it hard to lose the extra weight gained. Breast-feeding helps be-

cause of the extra energy demanded, but it takes a new mother a big effort to start exercising when she is exhausted from lack of sleep. Preparing food for a family puts temptation in the way of slimmers and it is difficult to stop nibbling or to resist finishing off the baby's leftovers.

Middle-age spread has more to do with life-style than with the slight drop in the resting metabolic rate (causing you to spend less calories as energy). This is the time of creeping obesity. You may have been able to eat whatever you liked when you were younger, but now the same kind of diet seems to turn to fat. It doesn't seem fair.

Perhaps you have more chances to eat in restaurants — it is probable you are becoming less active. It has been estimated that for every decade after the age of twenty there is a 10 percent reduction in resting metabolic calorie requirements. So if your eating habits do not change and if you don't make a conscious and consistent effort to increase activity and exercise, your fat layer will tend to increase.

As you get older, newspapers, telephone directories, and street maps suddenly seem more difficult to read. Bending closer doesn't seem to help, but backing away does. Presbyopia, or stiffening of the crystalline lens of the eye, causing loss of close focus, is the reason. Reading glasses or bifocals will help you get your life back into focus. Hearing may lose sensitivity with age; high frequency tones are less perceptible for many after the age of fifty.

Our body muscles lose size and strength as we get older, as we have seen, but it is disuse rather than aging that is to blame. At the menopause, when the feminine hormone estrogen diminishes, skin becomes less elastic, breasts shrink, muscle tone lessens, and bones may become weaker. Studies suggest that even modest physical activity can prevent the expected age-dependent rate of bone demineralization. There's a lot of truth in the old saying: if you don't want to lose it — use it!

In the elderly, it is likely that physical deterioration arises from decreasing physical activity rather than advancing years and is therefore potentially reversible. You can exercise, however old you are. But it does not need to be competitive. You can gain without pain. Maintain your physical condition with a good mix of activities, for example, a brisk walk every day and some suppleness and flexibility exercises. A yoga class that caters for older people is a safe way to stay supple. The capacity of the aged for physical exercise can be improved gradually with training, as it can be with the young. The over-sixties can improve both muscle power and tendon strength and also attain a healthier cardiovascular system.

Muscle is daily broken down and rebuilt through our lives, but with age, the muscle tends to deteriorate at a faster rate than it is remade, while the percentage of body fat increases. Exercise stimulates the build-up of muscle and physical fitness helps the elderly person to cope with the demands of living without fatigue, ensuring that life stays enjoyable and satisfying.

# YOUR WEIGHT AND YOU

**What should you weigh? And what's the difference between overweight and obesity? Before you embark on any slimming plan, these tables will help you set a target.**

What is "desirable" weight? To insurance companies, it is the range of weights that offer the greatest chance of survival during the period of insurance. The most widely publicized set of desirable weights are those issued by the Metropolitan Life Assurance Company, in the USA, in 1959.

At one time, weight charts used to be subdivided into frame size, but according to doctors this idea, although plausible, has no scientific foundation. Another way of assessing your size is the "body mass index" (see opposite).

The latest charts for desirable weight ranges, also published by Metropolitan Life and based on insurance experience of 4.2 million people between 1959 and 1979, have been revised *upwards*. The best weight for a long life is now up to 13 lb (6 kg) more than it used to be! However, the new range of weights does not necessarily reflect the ideal weight in terms of your *appearance*.

The chart given here is more realistic in this respect, and is the one given in the 1983 Obesity Report of the Royal College of Physicians, in Britain.

There's a difference between being overweight and being obese. In our chart, you will see that, for example, if you are 5 ft 4 in (1.62 m) tall, the acceptable weight range is between 108 lb (49 kg) and 138 lb (62 kg). You are overweight if you exceed this, but you won't be considered obese until you are 20 percent above it.

However, weight charts do not differentiate between fat and muscle, and it is the *fat* on your body that is the problem for slimmers. But how much fat is too much? The simplest test, although it is not very accurate, is to "pinch an inch." Sit down and pinch a fold of loose skin just above the waist. It is the distance between the fingers *through* the flesh that counts. If you pinch more than an inch, you have too much fat.

If you want to lose excessive body fat you need to reduce your calorie intake from food (and take more exercise), but you should not eat less than 1,000 calories a day.

You need to eat at least 800 calories a day or you will lose body protein, and therefore muscle mass. Even if you ate nothing but protein (and that would be a very bad diet) you would still lose protein. The reason? When you eat enough food to maintain weight, almost all your body's energy needs are met by normal carbohydrate, fat, and protein broken down from body tissues. The new protein you eat can be used to make new muscle tissue. But if you eat below 800 calories a day the protein is used as a source of energy and will not replace muscle losses.

Remember, exercise is just as important as dietary restriction in the management of obesity. The increase in energy expenditure which occurs during the activity may be quite small, but highly significant if it happens every day. And it is also thought possible that exercise stimulates the metabolism even after you have finished your exertions.

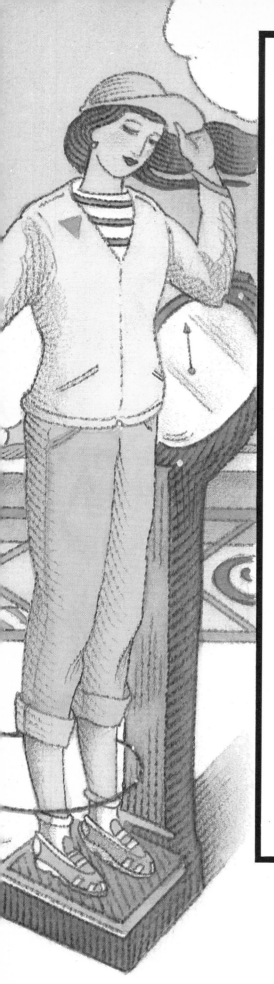

# HEIGHT AND WEIGHT CHARTS

## Women  Weight without clothes

| Height without shoes | | | Acceptable average | | Acceptable weight range | | Obese | |
|---|---|---|---|---|---|---|---|---|
| ft | in | m | lb | kg | lb | kg | lb | kg |
| 4 | 10 | 1.48 | 102 | 46.5 | 92–119 | 42–54 | 143 | 65 |
| 4 | 11 | 1.50 | 104 | 47.0 | 94–122 | 43–55 | 146 | 66 |
| 5 | 0 | 1.52 | 107 | 48.5 | 96–125 | 44–57 | 150 | 68 |
| 5 | 1 | 1.56 | 110 | 50.4 | 99–128 | 45–58 | 152 | 70 |
| 5 | 2 | 1.58 | 113 | 51.3 | 102–131 | 46–59 | 154 | 71 |
| 5 | 3 | 1.60 | 116 | 52.6 | 105–134 | 48–61 | 161 | 73 |
| 5 | 4 | 1.62 | 120 | 54.0 | 108–138 | 49–62 | 166 | 74 |
| 5 | 5 | 1.66 | 123 | 56.8 | 111–142 | 51–65 | 170 | 78 |
| 5 | 6 | 1.68 | 128 | 58.1 | 114–146 | 52–66 | 175 | 79 |
| 5 | 7 | 1.70 | 132 | 60.0 | 118–150 | 53–67 | 180 | 80 |
| 5 | 8 | 1.72 | 136 | 61.3 | 122–154 | 55–69 | 185 | 83 |
| 5 | 9 | 1.76 | 140 | 64.0 | 126–158 | 58–72 | 190 | 86 |
| 5 | 10 | 1.78 | 144 | 65.3 | 130–163 | 59–74 | 196 | 89 |
| 5 | 11 | 1.80 | 148 | 67.1 | 134–168 | 60–76 | 202 | 92 |
| 6 | 0 | 1.82 | 152 | 69.0 | 138–173 | 62–78 | 208 | 94 |
| **BMI** | | | **20.8** | | **18.7–23.8** | | **28.6** | |

## Men  Weight without clothes

| Height without shoes | | | Acceptable average | | Acceptable weight range | | Obese | |
|---|---|---|---|---|---|---|---|---|
| ft | in | m | lb | kg | lb | kg | lb | kg |
| 5 | 2 | 1.58 | 123 | 55.8 | 112–141 | 51–64 | 169 | 77 |
| 5 | 3 | 1.60 | 127 | 57.6 | 115–144 | 52–65 | 173 | 78 |
| 5 | 4 | 1.62 | 130 | 58.6 | 118–148 | 53–66 | 178 | 79 |
| 5 | 5 | 1.66 | 133 | 60.6 | 121–152 | 55–69 | 182 | 83 |
| 5 | 6 | 1.68 | 136 | 61.7 | 124–156 | 56–71 | 187 | 85 |
| 5 | 7 | 1.70 | 140 | 63.5 | 128–161 | 58–73 | 193 | 88 |
| 5 | 8 | 1.72 | 145 | 65.0 | 132–166 | 59–74 | 199 | 89 |
| 5 | 9 | 1.76 | 149 | 68.0 | 136–170 | 62–77 | 204 | 92 |
| 5 | 10 | 1.78 | 153 | 69.4 | 140–174 | 64–79 | 209 | 95 |
| 5 | 11 | 1.80 | 158 | 71.0 | 144–179 | 65–80 | 215 | 96 |
| 6 | 0 | 1.82 | 162 | 72.6 | 148–184 | 66–82 | 221 | 98 |
| 6 | 1 | 1.86 | 166 | 75.8 | 152–189 | 69–86 | 227 | 103 |
| 6 | 2 | 1.88 | 171 | 77.6 | 156–194 | 71–88 | 233 | 106 |
| 6 | 3 | 1.90 | 176 | 79.3 | 160–199 | 73–90 | 239 | 108 |
| 6 | 4 | 1.92 | 181 | 81.0 | 164–204 | 75–93 | 245 | 112 |
| **BMI** | | | **22.0** | | **20.1–25.0** | | **30.0** | |

*Body Mass Index (BMI)* is another way of assessing your size and is calculated by dividing your weight in kg by your height² in meters. (Thus if you weigh 56.8 kg (123 lb) and are 1.66 m (5 ft 5 in) tall the sum would be $\frac{56.8}{1.66 \times 1.66} = 20.5$)

Among normal men and women the index lies between about 20 and 25 and this corresponds to about 14 to 21 percent body fat for men and 24 to 31 percent body fat for women. Women champion distance runners are usually thin, having an index of about 19 with only 15 percent body fat.

A survey by the American Cancer Society concludes that a value of between 20 to 25 is associated with lowest mortality rates for both men and women.

# The Body Beautiful Through The Ages

Changing times bring changing tastes. The most desirable body shape for women has altered throughout our history, and in different countries and cultures. The modern preference for slenderness seems so strong that you might think it is and was a universal ideal. But this is far from true. In medieval times, the focus was on the rounded belly — functional in a period of high mortality, when constant pregnancy was necessary to keep the population stable. Women are natural endomorphs (having a rounded shape), say experts, and it is normal to have a body type that is softly curved. Until early in the twentieth century, Venus was always painted as an endomorph, moon-faced, pear-shaped, and well-fleshed out. It is only in the last sixty years that fatness seems to have faded as the hallmark of feminine appeal.

Fertility goddesses were bound to have bulging stomachs and be heavy breasted, of course. But those classical goddesses of Greece and Rome were no lightweights either. Statuesque they most certainly were. The Venus de Milo could never be described as small, while the Venus Callipyge gave us the word "callipygian," meaning to have a very well-endowed rear end. The Renaissance beauties painted by Titian and Georgione were definitely fleshy and broad-beamed, while Rubens' gorgeous nudes are overweight to modern eyes.

Restoration ladies were generously moulded. The poet Robert Herrick described his picture of the ideal woman of the period: "Black and rowling is her eye, Double chinn'd and forehead high."

The Regency belle wore girlish but erotically revealing clothes. Seldom have women worn less in public. When one magistrate heard that young ladies wore "bosom friends," to aid their natural shape, he cried: "Thank heavens they still wear *something*!" But not every admired figure was slender. Lady Hamilton, Nelson's Dearest Emma, said to be one of the most beautiful women of her generation, was undoubtedly plump, a rather full-blown rose, flamboyant but fat.

In the early nineteenth century, the feminine ideal was a cross between an angel and a child. Physical slightness and fragility were admired; to look helpless and useless was essential for a high social standing. To look fit and "in rude health" was considered lower class and coarse.

Mid-Victorian men were thrilled by plump, white, sloping shoulders. Their ideal woman had a tightly corseted handspan waist and, by 1860, steel-hooped crinolines supporting skirts like huge tea-cosies, which made her look like a majestic ship sailing proudly ahead. During the late Victorian period, interest centered on the rear end, exposed in the can-can and exaggerated by the bustle.

The Edwardian beauty was a mature figure with a voluptuous shape molded by a fearsome corset into a full, rounded bottom, narrow S-bend waist, and as large a bosom as nature and artifice would permit. With head thrown back, long swan neck, and magnificent shoulders, she was undoubtedly plump. Even twenty-year-olds tried to look forty. Hourglass curves and heavy thighs were admired.

It wasn't until the 1920s that women finally stopped trying to look like women — they preferred to be boys. The new erotic zone was the leg, accentuated in flesh-coloured silk or rayon stockings. Flat-chested, thin, low-waisted, short-skirted, outrageously different from anything that had gone before, the Twenties' Flapper wore "correctors" and "flatteners" to bind her breasts and look acceptably immature. The body looked like a flattened tube as wide at the waist as at the hips. With boyish hair cuts, too, it was a bid for freedom. It was also the beginning of slimming.

By the 1930s, a slightly more womanly woman was back again, with fluid bias-cut clothes accentuating gentle curves. Women turned their backs on Twenties' frivolities — literally — backs were bare to the waist, with skirts following the shape of the hips. Skirts cut on the cross clung the better.

*The womanly curves admired by Rubens were exaggerated by 19th-century fashions.*

The Fifties ideal woman had prominent breasts; Bardot and Marilyn Monroe had the shapes most women envied. Padded bras and conical bra cups gave the less well-endowed the chance to be fashionable. Monroe, like Jane Russell, another bosomy star, was well covered. The exaggerated feminine shape, all curves and rounded flesh, was to be replaced as an ideal by the Swinging Sixties' adolescent shape, with little waist and straight, almost boyish hips. Not everyone could be a Twiggy, but the trousers and unisex fashions demanded slimness. Mini skirts put slim legs into the spotlight. Being plump meant you couldn't compete at all.

Today, it is fashionable to be slender, but not fragile. The ideal woman of the Eighties has muscles. It is the athletic type who is most admired, and to get the right shape, you work at it with exercise and sport and healthy food. Corsets and girdles are banished.

For once the feminine ideal is to be fit and healthy.

## SOME MYTHS AND TRUTHS ABOUT FAT

**Myth:** Pinching, kneading, and slapping helps to disperse bulges.

**Truth:** Your body is not made of modeling clay and the only person truly affected by a massage (in terms of energy expenditure and fat loss) is the person doing the kneading. "Increasing the circulation" in an area of the body you wish to spot-reduce by pinching will only bring bruises.

**Myth:** You can melt off unwanted weight by sweating in saunas or plastic exercise suits.

**Truth:** When you are hot, you lose water by sweating and this fluid loss can result in a temporary weight loss and slight reduction in inches. But this all returns to normal as soon as you have a drink and your body regains its water levels.

**Myth:** You can get rid of cellulite by massage and special diets, or by rubbing in "reducing" creams.

**Truth:** Cellulite is the name given to lumpy uneven fat on the hips, thighs and upper arms but it *is* just fat. Biopsy studies made by pathologists of fat from people with dimply, lumpy fat tissue and those with ordinary unlumpy fatty tissue showed no difference in chemical composition of the fat cells. The fact that groups of fat cells are separated by folds of fibrous tissue into pockets is probably a culmination of age and obesity. Do not waste money on extraordinary "cures."

*The "ideal shapes" of the 20s and 30s reappeared in the 50s and 60s, as typified by Marilyn Monroe and Twiggy.*

THE BEST
THINGS

IN LIFE

We are what we eat, so we are told. The right kind of diet is essential for health, beauty, and a slim figure, as well as playing an important role in preventing disease and contributing to a longer life expectancy.

Times have changed and so has our attitude to food. Even nutritionists and teachers are having to rethink their guidelines. So what's good and not-so-good about our diet in the 1980s and are you up to date on the newest nutritional recommendations?

## Eat less fat

The biggest killer disease in the West is heart disease. Looking into causes, doctors found that an important factor is the concentration of fatty substances in the bloodstream, one of which is cholesterol.

For slimmers, it is important to remember that fat has more than double the calories of carbohydrates and cutting calories by reducing your fat intake could help your weight problem as well as your general health and well-being.

Cut down on *all* the fat you eat, in particular the animal and dairy fats. This means eating no more than 3 oz (75–85 g) of fat a day for women, 4 oz (100–115 g) of fat a day for men. So where do you begin? Write down a list of everything you normally eat in a day and see where you can cut down, with the help of the following tips. Here is a list of foods with the amount of fat contained in an average portion to give you an idea.

| Food | Portion | Grams of fat |
|---|---|---|
| Avocado pear | ½ medium | 11 |
| Bacon, streaky, broiled | 2 rashers | 9 |
| Beef, lean roast (fat removed) | 2 thin slices | 7 |
| Butter | 2 tsp | 8 |
| Cake, fruit | 1 slice | 8 |
| Cheese, cheddar | 2 oz (50 g) | 16 |
| Chicken, roast (no skin) | 3 thin slices | 4 |
| Chocolate | 1 small bar | 15 |
| Cookies, sweet | 2 small | 6 |
| Doughnut | 1 | 8 |
| Egg, boiled | 1 | 6 |
| Egg, fried | 1 | 10 |
| Ham, lean | 2 thin slices | 4 |
| Hamburger, broiled | 2 oz (50 g) size | 7 |
| Herring | 1 | 20 |
| Ice cream | 2 scoops | 8 |
| Lamb, lean roast | 2 thin slices | 6 |
| Liver, fried | 3 thin slices | 10 |
| Low-fat spread | 2 tsp | 4 |
| Margarine | 2 tsp | 8 |
| Mayonnaise | 1 level tbsp | 12 |
| Milk, skimmed | 10 fl oz (275 ml) | 0 |
| Milk, whole | 10 fl oz (275 ml) | 11 |
| Mushrooms, fried | 10 button size | 11 |
| Oil | 1 tbsp | 15 |
| Pastry | 2 tart cases | 12 |
| Peanuts, salted | 1 oz (25 g) | 12 |
| Pork chop, lean | 1 | 5 |
| Potato chips | 4 oz (110 g) | 11 |
| Sausage, broiled | 1 large size | 10 |
| Trout | 1 | 12 |

(With permission of *Successful Slimming* magazine.)

● **Spread** butter or margarine more thinly by softening it first, and scrape off surplus, or switch to low-calorie spreads if you are a slimmer. But remember, soft margarines, although high in polyunsaturates (thought to have a beneficial anti-cholesterol effect on the body), have the same amount of calories as other margarines and butter. Only low-fat spreads (which contain almost four times as much water) have fewer calories, but they are not necessarily high in poly-unsaturated fat. One product sells on "health," the other on "slimming."

● **Give up** using cream and try natural yogurt instead. Switch to skimmed milk. Because it has a low-fat content, it also has far fewer calories than whole milk and can be a big saving for slimmers.

● **Resist** the temptation to fill up on hard cheeses, which are high in both fat and calories. Try the new lower-fat varieties and soft skimmed-milk cheeses, cottage or curd cheese, but not cream cheese. Always check the fat content on the label before buying.

● **Choose** lean cuts of meat and always cut off visible fat, and cut the skin off poultry before eating. Pork, lamb, and beef are more fatty than chicken or fish, which is particularly recommended, but not fried in batter. If you eat more than 2–4 oz (50–110 g) of red meat three or four times a week, or have fried foods more than three times a week, you could be eating too much saturated fat for your health.

● **Consider** that even a lean sirloin steak can be 10 percent fat, and go easy on other fatty meats or dishes such as bacon, salami, delicatessen sausage products, luncheon meat, sausage rolls, and pâtés.

● **Stop** frying because fried food contains a large amount of fat. Broil instead and let the fat drain away. Mop up sausages and chops (both fatty foods) with absorbent paper towels before eating.

● **Brown** hamburger meat first in a nonstick pan without added fat or oil, then drain off the fatty liquid before adding other ingredients. When making stews, a good way to remove fat is to put the dish in the refrigerator overnight, then lift off the solidified fat next day.

● **Try** eating more dishes with higher carbohydrate content and use meat just for flavouring. For instance: spaghetti and other pasta dishes, or paella.

● **Remember** that cakes, pastries, cookies, chocolate, and ice cream are surprisingly rich in fat as well as sugar. There is hidden fat in gravy, sauces, and mayonnaise.

● **Go easy** on nuts, chips, savory crackers and nibbles.

● **Dress** salads with low-fat/low-calorie dressings or make your own with yogurt, herbs, and mustard. Try replacing half the usual oil with tomato juice and use more herb vinegars or lemon juice.

● **Thicken** soups with pureed vegetables, yogurt, or skimmed-milk powder instead of cream.

## FAT AND YOUR HEART

Although long suspected, it was only recently that a major drug trial provided the first irrefutable evidence that lowering blood cholesterol levels lessens the risk of heart disease (see page 10). The results of a study of 4,000 patients by the US National Institutes of Health have so convinced heart disease experts on both sides of the Atlantic that they are now suggesting widespread screening to identify people with high cholesterol levels, coupled with active treatment by diet or diet plus drug therapy when they are discovered.

This could involve as many as one in three of the population, and the experts propose that individuals should be screened every ten years from the age of thirty, and that doctors should test all the members of a family if one of them is found to have high blood cholesterol.

So far, even the organizers of the US study have stopped short of recommending diets for everyone, even those not at risk. But their evidence reinforces the feeling of many nutritionists that we should *all* eat a lower-fat diet, with less fatty meat, fewer eggs and dairy foods, and eat more *polyunsaturates*, especially those found in fish.

## WHICH FAT IS WHICH?

Are you puzzled about the fat *v* margarine contest? Are animal fats all bad and vegetable-based fats all good? Although the seesaw goes up and down depending on which food lobby gets the most publicity, the consensus of opinion by the medical profession seems to be this:

*Yes,* it might well be a good idea to substitute saturated fats (lard, butter) with oils and margarines containing polyunsaturated fatty acids, in a modest way, as an acceptable measure in devising a more healthy, low-fat diet.

*No,* you do not have to give up butter altogether, if you like it, provided you keep an eye on your total fat and calorie intake.

Butter actually only amounts to 12 percent of the fat eaten in a normal diet. Meat and meat products amount to 27 percent, other edible fats and oils, 12 percent, milk and dairy produce, 19 percent, margarine, 13 percent and other foods, 18 percent. (Source: MAFF. Sources of fat in UK foods 1981.)

*Look twice* at the label before you buy your margarine, if you are using it as a substitute for butter, because many margarines are just as high in saturated fat. Look out for ones claiming to be high in polyun-saturates, and avoid the ones containing "blended vegetable oils."

Olive oil is low in both polyun-saturated and saturated fat but high in neutral monosaturated fat, so it is considered healthy for cooking.

Low-fat spreads are lower in calories, so they are useful for slimmers. But they still contain over 40 percent saturated fats.

# Take less salt

The evidence that too much salt can be a health risk because of its link with high blood pressure is growing – and we eat about twenty times more than we need.

A high intake of salt can give rise to hypertension in some people (particularly if there is a family history) and it has been estimated that as many as one-third of the population could be affected.

High blood pressure develops

over a number of years without noticeable symptoms. It is accepted as one of the major health risks (along with excess weight, smoking, and lack of exercise) leading to a higher incidence of strokes and heart disease. In fact, the World Health Organization recommends that people should try to have their blood pressure checked regularly from childhood onward. More than half of those found to have high blood pressure were unaware that they had a problem – and thus did not take steps to control it.

Too much salt in childhood might well lead to high blood pressure in later life, it is feared, so it is not a good idea to add salt to baby foods. A bland diet is probably better so that children don't get a taste for salty foods.

Salt is more of a risk to women with a family history of hypertension, but also to women who are overweight or have passed the menopause, when the protective effects against heart disease of the hormone estrogen have ended.

An excess of salt can alter the biochemical balance of your body, favoring changes that gradually help to raise blood pressure, so patients under treatment for hypertension are usually advised to cut down on salt as well as to lose excess weight. Diuretics increase the amount of urine and thus help to reduce sodium in the body.

Recent research by the Blood Pressure Unit at Charing Cross Hospital Medical School, London, showed that patients suffering from moderate hypertension could bring their blood pressure down to normal without drugs simply by shunning the salt shaker. A small Chinese take-away meal analysed at the hospital harboured about $2\frac{1}{2}$ teaspoons of salt, about three times as much as a blood pressure patient should have in a day!

That's the problem. Salt seems to be in just about everything we put into our mouths. For a healthy life, we require a certain amount of sodium a day, of course, but $\frac{1}{4}$ teaspoon would do!

As salt is contained in so many packaged and instant foods, it is often impossible to know just how much salt you are eating. Labeling the sodium content would be useful. In the meantime, try to banish salt from the table and use less when preparing food.

● **Cut down** on salty foods such as

---

## Good diets and bad diets

There are no good foods or bad foods, just good diets and not-so-good diets. For years we were told to give up bread, potatoes, and sugar as part of low-carbohydrate diets. We were encouraged to drink plenty of milk and be sure to eat lots of dairy foods and juicy steaks in an attempt to "balance" our food habits, which is now counter to current medical opinion.

The "balance" was meant to guard against deficiency diseases of protein, vitamins, and minerals, which are no longer likely in our affluent society. The message now is to eat less fat, less salt, less sugar, more complex carbohydrates, such as potatoes and wholewheat cereals, and more fruit and vegetables.

### NOT SO HEALTHY EATING
**Breakfast**
fried egg, bacon, sausage, and fried bread (fried in lard); tea or coffee with whole milk and sugar; 2 slices of white toast with lots of butter and marmalade
**Lunch**
meat pie and french fries; baked sponge pudding and custard; tea or coffee with whole milk and sugar
**Snack**
packet of chips; cup of tea or coffee with chocolate cookies
**Dinner**
lamb chop or hamburger with roast potatoes, peas and gravy; apple pie with cream; tea or coffee with whole milk and sugar; slice of cheddar cheese with crackers, butter

### A HEALTHY WAY TO EAT
**Breakfast**
wholewheat cereal or muesli (no sugar) with chopped up dried apricot, or banana and skimmed milk; small glass of orange juice; tea or coffee with skimmed milk (no sugar); slice of wholewheat bread or toast with scraping of butter or margarine and a teaspoon of marmalade
**Lunch**
baked potato with chicken livers and mushrooms; mixed salad; piece of fresh fruit; tea or coffee with skimmed milk, no sugar
**Snack**
slice of wholewheat bread; little cheese spread and chopped celery; sparkling mineral water
**Dinner**
wholewheat pasta with tuna and tomato; side salad of grated carrot, diced turnip, or other root vegetable like celeriac; crunchy cabbage; low-calorie dressing; baked apple with sultanas or nuts, cinnamon; natural yogurt

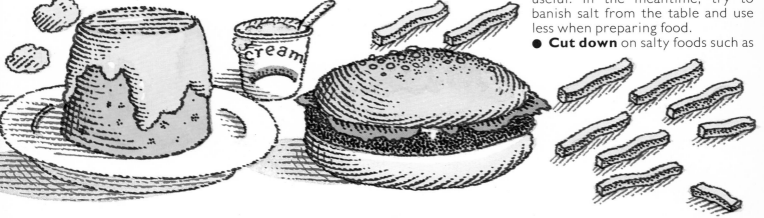

bacon, salted peanuts, cheese, ham, luncheon meat, chopped pork, salami, and sausage. Other foods with a very high salt content are: cereals, smoked cod, smoked haddock, smoked salmon, shellfish, instant potato, olives in brine, pickles, tomato ketchup, stock cubes, and baking powder. Even custard powder, self-raising flour, and bread contain salt, and it can be found in everything from hamburgers to butter, water crackers and spaghetti. A reasonable helping of some breakfast cereals provides about a quarter of your daily needs.

● **Look at labels** because, although the law does not insist on salt being listed, you can sometimes tell there is a salt content if it contains the following: baking powder, baking soda, sodium bicarbonate or bicarbonate of soda, brine, monosodium glutamate, sodium benzoate, sodium sulphite, sodium hydroxide, sodium cyclamate or sodium alginate.

One thing that may help protect against salt-induced hypertension is to increase the intake of potassium. Found in many fresh foods such as citrus fruits, watercress, all green leafy vegetables, potatoes, bananas, and even asparagus, potassium counteracts the effects of sodium.

# Cut down on sugar

Pure, white, and deadly is the famous description of refined sugar, placed firmly on the list of dietary undesirables, and this is one area where times haven't changed! This sweet carbohydrate has long been thought unnecessary for a healthy diet and, because it is high in calories without having any other nutrient benefits, it needs to be restricted on any slimming plan.

In the last hundred years, the amount of carbohydrate in our diet has gone down, but the amount of sugar has gone up, detrimental both to our figures and our teeth. It is true that sugar consumption is gradually declining, from about 110 lb (53 kg) per head per year in 1974 to 94 lb (43 kg) in 1982, in a trend away from sweet foods, but this is still an enormous amount.

In fact, doctors are advising us to halve our intake, restricting sugar in the form of confectionery, soft drinks, and snacks as much as possible.

Sugar stimulates the body to lay down fat, say some experts. A diet high in sugar is directly associated with adult-onset diabetes, and although the exact role of sugar in contributing to coronary heart disease is not clear, obesity and diabetes are associated with heart disease, and sugar may have an additional effect.

The more sugar you eat, the more dental problems you are likely to incur. The bacteria in plaque (a substance which forms on teeth quite soon after brushing and which gradually thickens into a sticky layer containing millions of bacteria) changes sugar into acid which dissolves and eventually makes holes in the outer enamel layer of the teeth.

After about one to two hours, the saliva in the mouth is able to neutralize the acid. But the more frequently sugar is eaten, the more often the teeth come under attack. So keep any sweet treats to mealtimes and try not to consume sugary snacks throughout the day.

Sugar is hidden in everything from baked beans, sauces, and soups to cereals, crispbreads, and even baby rusks. Sweets are the biggest offenders. A chocolate bar is more than 50 percent sugar, some pickles and chutneys are 30 percent, tomato ketchup has 22 percent sugar, ice cream about 20 percent and even a cola drink contains 10 percent.

● **Read labels** Contents are in descending order, so if sugar is listed near the beginning, there is a lot in the food. Look out for sugar-free muesli, canned fruit in natural juice, and low-calorie diet drinks.

● **Stop** adding sugar to tea, coffee, fruit, or cereal. If you cannot do without some sweetening, try artificial sweeteners.

● **Try** to cut down on sweets, chocolate, cakes, cookies, desserts, and sweet drinks. Use fruit for desserts – cubes or balls of melon mixed with strawberries, raspberries, or other soft fruit, for example, or sliced bananas tossed in lemon juice with black or green grapes. Do not peel apples, pears, or grapes because the skin is a valuable source of fiber.

● **Energy boosters** We sometimes crave an ice cream, cake, or cookie when we are feeling low and need a quick energy boost. But for every sugar "high," there's a corresponding "low" when the blood sugar levels return to normal. For a slow, steady, and healthier increase in energy, nutritionists advocate complex carbohydrates such as bread, pasta, and beans. And new research has shown, surprisingly, that some carbohydrates can raise blood sugar levels faster than a chocolate bar, and that an apple or orange has the same effect on blood sugar as an ice cream!

According to American tests, ranking foods *in order* according to their effect on blood glucose levels, it would seem to be wiser to reach for a carrot than a toffee! The foods absorbed most quickly into the bloodstream were: parsnips, carrots, honey, cornflakes, white rice, wholewheat bread, instant potatoes, white bread, a candy bar, brown rice, raisins, bananas, sugar, apples, ice cream, yogurt, tomato

soup, pasta, baked beans, chickpeas, lentils, and peanuts.

A *sweet tooth* is another way of saying you have a sugar craving, which has been many a dieter's downfall. Like any other habit, it can be hard to break. One way is to give yourself a sugar holiday: give up *all* sugar, and anything sweet for a week, and try to experience the real taste of food. Then keep to natural fruit and fruit juice for adding a touch of sweetness.

## Eat more fiber

Dietary fiber is the indigestible part of fruit, vegetables, and cereals – a residue of plant cell walls that gets passed straight through the body. Doctors believe we should eat more fiber-containing foods to help prevent bowel disease, constipation, and possibly heart disease, gall bladder disease, varicose veins, piles, and obesity.

Fiber adds bulk to your meals and acts as a bulking agent during digestion, helping to prevent constipation, but leaving behind very few calories. Because fiber is only partly digested, most of it passes through the intestines unchanged, where it absorbs water, increases the bulk of the undigested food, and helps the muscles of the colon to work efficiently.

In Britain during World War II, a lean but healthy period for food, people ate about 1 to 1½ oz (32 to 40 g) of fiber per day – which is only slightly less than vegetarians eat on average. The daily norm now is only ¾ oz (20 g), considered far too low for our health.

There's fiber and fiber. Bran is one form called lignin, which is effective at relieving constipation. Another – the gums and mucilages found in peas, beans and lentils – helps to control blood sugar. This is important both to diabetics and slimmers because it gives a feeling of fullness, which is useful if you are overweight. The pectins are

natural gelling agents found in fruits and are said to be helpful in reducing cholesterol in the bloodstream. While pentose (see page 12) may protect against bowel cancer.

Too much added bran can be harmful because you risk reducing mineral absorption (zinc, iron and calcium) into the body, because bran (as well as being high in fiber) is also a source of phytate, a substance known to prevent some minerals from being absorbed. One to two tablespoons of bran have been shown to reduce calcium absorption. This is worrying for older people, since not only are they more likely to get constipation, but also osteoporosis, a bone disease found in the elderly, especially women after the menopause, which can be caused or aggravated by calcium deficiency.

So the healthiest way to increase fiber in your diet is to eat more whole foods such as fruit and fresh vegetables, wholegrain cereals and pulses. Such a diet is much more healthy than a more typical Western diet that is rich in fat, milk foods, sweet cakes, biscuits, and refined foods and low in fiber. Simply adding a sprinkling of bran may add a little fiber, but it will not alter the unhealthy balance.

Bread and potatoes, long the staple items in the Western diet, were wrongly classified as "baddies" for years because of the popularity of low-carbohydrate diets, now considered the worst way to slim! Bread is an important source of fiber in our diet and all types contain useful amounts, although wholewheat bread provides more than three times the amount of fiber that white does.

Potatoes, besides being extremely important as a source of Vitamin C, also contribute 3 to 4 percent of our protein, and provide a useful amount of fiber, especially if you eat the skins.

Good sources of fiber to include in your diet: raspberries, baked beans, dried figs, wholewheat breakfast cereals or bran-based breakfast cereals, blackberries, stewed apricots, prunes, haricot and kidney beans, sweet corn, spinach, nuts, pulses, wholewheat pasta, brown rice.
*Wind warning!* A sudden large increase in fiber can lead to

flatulence, so increase the amount of fiber in your diet little by little over a period of time.

## Eat plenty of fruit and vegetables

Healthy eating means fresh ingredients, and a great variety of different foods in order to get all the right nutrients. Natural vegetables and fruit are vital to the diet because of the trace elements, vitamins, and minerals, which your body needs to function efficiently, as well as for their fiber content.

Vitamin C, being water soluble, needs to be topped up every day. It is the one vitamin you should consciously remember because it is easily destroyed by cooking and bad handling. Prepare salads just before eating, because storage and chopping causes Vitamin C losses. Cook vegetables in a minimum of water for a minimum of time and don't keep them standing. When boiling potatoes, as much as 60 percent of Vitamin C may be lost in the water so use it for soups, stews and gravy. Even better, bake potatoes in their skins for the benefits of fiber, as well as preserving nutrients.

Vitamin C helps the iron contained in other foods to be absorbed by the body, an important point for women, who lose iron during menstruation.

Because they also contain a lot of water, fruit and vegetables are important to slimmers, since they give bulk without many calories.

## What about protein?

If you eat excessive amounts of protein, the body simply converts it to fat and stores it as fat. You actually only need about 1½ oz (45 g) of protein a day for health. (Food isn't just solid protein, remember. For example 3½ oz (100 g) of lean roast sirloin is only about a quarter protein and slightly less than 10 per cent fat.) Protein from animal sources is usually accompanied by large quantities of fat. Protein from vegetables (lentils, peas, beans, bread) are a good source, and usually cheaper.

High-protein slimming diets are not a good idea, because they will also tend to be high in fat and low in carbohydrates.

# Eating for health

If you want to keep yourself and your family healthy and increase the fiber in your diet, what does it actually mean in terms of quantities and shopping?

Well, the 1 oz (30 g) of fiber you should aim to eat in a day could come from a portion of wholewheat breakfast cereal, four small portions of leafy vegetables, one portion of peas, one medium potato and two or three slices of wholewheat bread.

## Breakfasts

Instead of a cooked breakfast, introduce a variety of fiber-rich bran-based or wholewheat breakfast cereals. You could try making up your own muesli, or add dried apricots, raisins or sultanas to any mixture of cereals – you don't have to stick to just one type in your dish. Have a piece of fruit or fresh juice.

## Lunches

If you are out at work, take sandwiches using wholewheat bread – wholewheat, not brown. The fillings depend on whether or not you are trying to slim. For instance, sardine and tomato, cottage cheese and cucumber, shrimp and salad, egg and cress with low-calorie dressing, are all about 250 calories a sandwich or less. Date and nut with low-fat cheese would be about 300 plus calories. Peanut butter with shrimps or chicken or raisins are also around 300 calories. Eat a piece of fresh fruit, too.

## Evening meals

Enjoy wholewheat pasta dishes; try recipes using spinach, a good source of fiber. Its legendary iron content is rather a myth. Iron from meat is a better source, and more easily absorbed by the body if taken at the same time as Vitamin C, from vegetables or fruit juice perhaps. Use a baked potato as the base for a meal, adding different ingredients, such as chicken and sweet corn, sardines and salad, scrambled egg and tomato. If you want to have salad, be a bit more imaginative about the ingredients. For instance, the odd lettuce leaf or two, with cucumber, watercress, and a spring onion, won't give you much fiber. Try instead salads made with shredded white cabbage, carrot, chopped celery, Chinese cabbage leaves, mushrooms, chopped green pepper, cauliflower sprigs, grated parsnips, diced turnip, beetroot, apple, cooked peas, new potatoes, sweetcorn, green beans (cooked) or canned red kidney beans. Add shredded chicken or turkey, tuna or shrimps, cottage cheese or ham. Use low-calorie salad dressings or make your own using tomato juice, low-fat natural yogurt, and mustard, herbs and herb vinegars, lemon juice.

For desserts, mix up your own varieties of fruity yogurts with low-fat natural yogurt, artificial sweetener, and fresh fruit such as raspberries, blackcurrants, a chopped

LUNCH BOX 1  350 calories, suitable for a woman. Egg spread made from 1 chopped hard-boiled egg, ½ oz (15 g) grated cheddar or crumbled stilton cheese, 2 tsp low-fat natural yogurt, seasoning, chopped watercress leaves. 2 crispbreads. 2 tomatoes. 1 broiled beef sausage. 1 small apple, pear, peach, or orange.

apple, or raisins. Baked apples make good low-calorie, high-fiber desserts. Serve with cinnamon, dried apricots, dates, raisins or nuts, and honey. Stewed fruit is also a good choice.

## Snacks

Baked beans are high in fiber (although they also contain quite a bit of sugar), so they are useful for a quick cooking; served with wholewheat toast, mashed potato, a little grated cheese, mushrooms, and eggs. Crispbreads containing a good percentage of bran are worth considering for a light meal, too.

## Lunch boxes

Packed lunches to take to work or school don't have to be boring and they can be ideal for slimmers because you control the calories.

Always make sandwiches with wholewheat bread and a scraping of low-fat spread (or polyunsaturated margarine).

Fill a small plastic container with salad and low-calorie dressing for a change. Take fresh fruit and a sugar-free fruit juice or low-calorie drink.

For nibbling, take carrot, cucumber, or strips of green pepper.

*Avoid* pies or anything with pastry, chips, chocolate, biscuits, a lot of hard cheese (high fat and high calorie).

## Weekend and holiday eating

Eating together with your family or friends, the last thing you want to do is eat something different, or have the bother of making two kinds of meals. So if you work during the week and you are trying to lose weight, it could be better to be stricter on weekdays, and save more of your calories to "spend" at the weekend.

In any case, healthy eating can be enjoyable so there's no reason why you have to cook the kind of food that is on list of "undesirables"!

Start collecting recipes for low-fat sauces, soups, and salad dressings. Since baked potatoes (or boiled), wholewheat pasta, and brown rice are nutritious sources of healthy fiber, these can be made into family-filling dishes with lower-fat sauces. Choose less-fatty cuts of meat and cut off all visible fat.

If the family *insist* on french fries, make bigger ones (less fat content) and cook them in polyunsaturated maize or sunflower oil at a very high temperature, drain, then blot on paper towels. Never cook with animal lard – it is a saturated fat.

Always have plenty of fruit and vegetables available and buy wholewheat bread rather than white or brown.

On holiday, slimming and healthy eating can be difficult if you are full- or half-board at a hotel. If you are self-catering, you can shop for just what you want and foreign markets can be fun with exotic and different fruit and vegetables to choose from.

But two weeks out of your year don't really matter, if you go back to a healthy, nutritious way of eating once you get back home.

LUNCH BOX 2  500 calories, suitable for a man or child.
3 slices of wholewheat bread, very lightly buttered and made into a double sandwich with 2 fillings:
*filling 1* ½ oz grated cheese and 1 tsp pickle.
*filling 2* sliced cucumber, tomato, mustard and cress, and 2 chopped dates. Fruit salad made by stewing 5 prunes, half a dried pear, and 2 dried apple rings.
Individual tub of low-fat natural yogurt.

# THE NEW DIETS

**A good diet isn't crash or cranky, but satisfies your moods and needs, reducing calories but not nutritive value.**

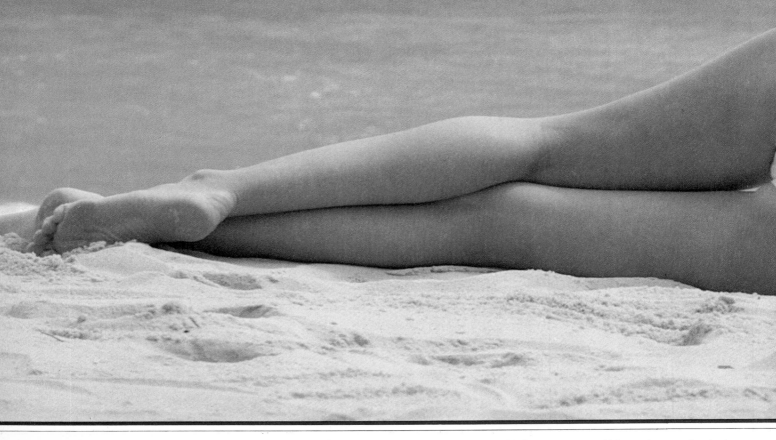

The days of the crash diets are over (or should be), because when it comes to losing excess weight, and keeping it off, they just don't work. You may well lose pounds but you are losing glycogen and water, not fat. Glycogen is a type of glucose, stored in solution in the liver and muscles to be available for energy when needed by the brain and body. This "muscle sugar" burns much faster than fat; an athlete can lose many pounds of it during exercise. Low-carbohydrate diets, which cut starches and sugar, have the effect of draining the body's glycogen reserves in the first week. At the same time, low glycogen levels trigger off hunger. So crash dieting, reducing starchy foods, will lead to short-term rapid weight losses, which are soon replaced.

Even if you eat a lot of other types of food, such as protein, you still have carbohydrate hunger because of the glycogen losses. Carbohydrates, the starchy nutrients, feed the glycogen stores in the body and raise the blood glucose level so that you feel satisfied. Losing glycogen leaves you feeling weak and depressed, and can lead to dizziness and irritability.

Despite what you may sometimes read in the newspapers, there is no magic metabolic mixture or diet to assure a more effective weight loss other than a good, nutritious, reduced-calorie diet. Grapefruits and passion fruit or pineapples do not spirit away your surplus flesh because of their special qualities. Fiber may be filling and good for your health, but it does not have any mystical qualities either.

Diets make you slim *only* if you change your life-style to include more exercise and activity, too, and modify your pattern of behavior when it comes to eating, so you have more chance of success in keeping the surplus weight off for good.

Weight loss by diet alone causes a significant loss of lean muscle tissue – which is most undesirable. If you lose weight slowly but surely on a sensible eating plan, and do exercise, you guard against losing muscle, and thus most of the weight loss will be fat tissue.

Most adults' body weight fluctuates only slightly during the year (unless you are in the yoyo slimming syndrome) even though it has been estimated that we eat on average about 1600 to 1900 lb (700 to 900 kg) of food in twelve months. This relative stability in body weight in people of normal weight seems very

impressive when you think how just a slight increase in food intake for some habitual slimmers can cause a substantial weight increase. It is the energy intake/expenditure sum that holds the balance. Only when the number of calories ingested as food exceeds your daily energy requirements do those excess calories get stored as fat in adipose tissue.

If you go on an extremely rigorous diet, which makes you feel low, you could well be spending even less energy. You will not have the vitality to be active. After several bouts of this kind of very restrictive dieting, your body begins to get wise. It sees the dieting as "famine," becomes more efficient, and your metabolic rate at rest could well decline. In the end you practically have to starve yourself in order to lose any weight

at all. It is a vicious circle getting you nowhere.

Fad diets can slow you down, damage your health, and are self-defeating. Good eating habits are the key to successful slimming, if, at the same time you do sufficient exercise, especially the sort that helps your cardiovascular function — it makes you sweat. For many slimmers, it is not the amount of food they eat that is the problem — they could well be eating less than thinner friends — but the fact that they are sedentary.

But even so, the diet dilemma isn't quite that simple. Some of us are good burners and some of us are slow burners. The old equation — that high calorie intake plus low calorie output equals a fat person — is now being questioned in the scientific laboratories.

At the Dunn Nutrition Unit in Cambridge, England, researchers are investigating the production of body heat (known as thermogenesis), which seems to take place mostly in certain "brown fat" cells, found between the shoulder blades and around the kidneys. Scientists are looking into the possibility of thermogenic drugs to switch up heat production in these brown fat cells and therefore use up surplus calories. So there could be some interesting developments in the slimming field in the next few years.

The following diets are based on healthy foods and are chosen to suit your moods and your life-style. They are examples of how you can reduce your intake of calories sensibly, so you can lose weight slowly and gradually giving you a chance to rethink your habits.

# The Fill Up With Fiber Diet

**(1200 calories a day)**
This is a kind of eating plan that is in line with the latest medical thinking about food and your health. A diet higher in complex carbohydrates and fiber and lower in fat and sugar is one of "the prudent diets" that doctors recommend. You certainly should not feel hungry or deprived and yet you will lose weight safely and consistently over a period of time.

Remember, fiber fills you up but you also have to make an effort to cut calories. So no fried food, restrict butter, margarine, cheese, and pastry. Be sure to drink plenty of water, tea, coffee or any low-calorie drink. Try to spread the high-fiber foods throughout the day rather than eating them all at breakfast.

If you are not used to eating a lot of fruit, vegetables, and bran cereals, take it easy and increase your fiber gradually. Plunging in to such a changed pattern of eating so suddenly could make you feel uncomfortable.

**Allowances:** Each day you are allowed 10 fl oz (275 ml) skimmed milk for tea and coffee. That is enough for about 7 cups. No sugar in drinks. Grams of fiber are given for each meal.

**Breakfasts:** Choose one each day. If you want to eat it in the evening rather than the morning, do so. But don't eat buns and cookies at mid-morning because you feel hungry.
**1** 5 heaped tbsps bran cereal or portion wholewheat cereal
5 fl oz (150 ml) skimmed milk
1 small chopped apple
2 chopped dried apricots (17 g)
**2** 2 slices wholewheat toast
2 level tsps butter or margarine
2 level tsps marmalade or jam or honey (7 g)
**3** 3 dried figs
½ melon filled with grapes
1 slice of wholewheat bread
1 level tsp butter or margarine (15 g)
**4** 5 chopped dates mixed with ½ oz (15 g) toasted chopped nuts
1 tsp honey
5 oz (150 g) low-fat natural yogurt (5 g)
**5** muesli made by mixing:
3 heaped tbsps oatmeal
1 heaped tbsp bran
1 level tbsp toasted flaked almonds
2 chopped dried apricots
5 fl oz (150 ml) skimmed milk (11 g)

**Main Meal 1:** This is a lightish meal, choose one each day.
**1** chicken salad made from:
2 oz (50 g) cooked chicken, no skin
shredded white cabbage
½ diced apple
4 walnut halves, chopped
2 chopped sticks celery
1 tbsp yogurt dressing
1 tbsp low-fat natural yogurt
dessert: 1 orange, 2 apricots (10 g)
**2** 1 wholewheat muffin split and toasted, topped with 2 sliced tomatoes then 1 oz (25 g) grated cheddar cheese or mozzarella cheese, broil and top with 1 slice well-broiled bacon
dessert: 1 apple or pear or orange (9 g)
**3** salad made by mixing:
2 oz (50 g) cooked lima beans
2 oz (50 g) cooked red kidney beans
4 oz (110 g) cooked cut green beans
chopped celery
4 chopped walnut halves
chopped onion
1 tbsp yogurt dressing
with 1 slice wholewheat bread (14 g)
**4** 3½ oz (100 g) cod steak (no bone) baked in a foil parcel with sliced onion, stock, and 1 sliced tomato
7 oz (200 g) baked potato
1 tbsp sour cream
large portion peas (10 g)
**5** open sandwich made with:
1 slice wholewheat bread
lettuce and cucumber slices
2 oz (50 g) peeled shrimps mixed with 1 tbsp yogurt dressing and 1 tsp tomato puree. Serve with lemon wedge
dessert: 5 oz (150 g) fresh or frozen raspberries
4 tbsp low-fat natural yogurt mixed with 2 tbsp orange juice (15 g)
**6** 10 fl oz (275 ml) can any low-calorie soup or make your own
1 slice wholewheat bread
dessert: ½ small melon filled with any soft fruit (10 g)
**7** 1 poached egg on:
6 oz (175 g) cooked spinach
4 oz (110 g) cooked spaghetti – preferably wholewheat
dessert: 4 dates (15 g)
**8** 3 sardines on 1 slice wholewheat toast
2 broiled tomatoes
dessert: fruit salad made from 1 orange, 1 grapefruit, and 6 grapes (9 g)
**9** 7 oz (200 g) baked potato filled with 3 heaped tbsp cooked sweet corn
salad of celery, cucumber, onion
dessert: 6 prunes or 3 dried figs (14 g)
**10** 6 oz (175 g) broiled filleted white fish served with 2 oz (50 g) black grapes

salad of lettuce, sliced cucumber, watercress, and 1 sliced orange
1 slice wholewheat bread (6 g)

**Main Meal 2:** These are rather more substantial meals, choose one each day.
**1** 2 lamb cutlets, broiled (no fat)
large portion boiled, mashed turnip
large portion cauliflower and 2 tbsp white sauce (5 g)
**2** 4 oz (110 g) pork fillet casseroled with onion, stock, seasoning, and 4 dried apricot halves
3 heaped tbsp cooked brown rice
large portion cooked broccoli, sprinkled with ½ oz (15 g) toasted chopped hazelnuts (12 g)
**3** 7 oz (200 g) trout, broiled and topped with ½ oz (15 g) toasted flaked almonds
large portion spinach
large portion sliced green beans
dessert: 1 peach or pear (13 g)
**4** 8 oz (225 g) chicken joint, skin removed and casseroled with onion, stock, carrots, tarragon, and seasoning
4 oz (110 g) boiled potatoes
large portion peas
large portion broccoli (12 g)
**5** 3 oz (75 g) roast/boiled lean ham
2 tbsp parsley sauce
3 oz (75 g) broad beans
large portion baby carrots
dessert: 4 fresh plums or 5 prunes
2 tbsp low-fat natural yogurt (10 g)
**6** 5 oz (150 g) veal cutlet, broiled and topped with 1 oz (25 g) mozzarella cheese and 1 sliced tomato
serve on a large portion spinach
2 broiled tomatoes (12 g)
**7** 4 oz (110 g) stewing beef casseroled with stock, onion, herbs, and seasoning
large portion red cabbage with onion and apple
5 oz (150 g) mashed potato, no butter
dessert: 1 pear or peach or apple (10 g)
**8** 3 oz (75 g) thinly sliced liver, broiled and topped with orange slices
large portion broccoli
3 oz (75 g) peas or broad beans
dessert: 2 slices fresh pineapple (or canned in water or natural juice, no syrup) and 1 sliced kiwi fruit (11 g)
**9** pasta salad made from:
2 oz (50 g) raw weight pasta shells, boiled
3 oz (75 g) poached and diced cod
diced celery and cucumber
3 oz (75 g) peas
dessert: 1 sliced orange (13 g)
**10** lamb kebab made with 4 oz (110 g) lean marinaded lamb, tiny tomatoes, red and green pepper and onion pieces
1 oz (25 g) (raw weight) brown rice, boiled and mixed with ½ oz (15 g) pistachio nuts, 1 oz (25 g) peas and 1 oz (25 g) sweet corn (6 g)

*A diet higher in complex carbohydrates and fiber; lower in fat and sugar.*

# The Indulge Your Cravings Diet

**(1200 calories a day)**
You don't have to become a diet martyr in order to lose weight. If you fancy a sweet treat or a glass of wine or something stronger, now and again, it is still possible to build it into a nutritious diet that helps you slim.

If you have enough control to know when to stop, then this diet could help you feel happier as you are losing weight. However, if one small chocolate is enough to make you scream to finish the box, try one of the other diets.

Recent research shows that chemical changes in the brain, set in motion by low-carbohydrate diets, can give you a sugar craving, or make it worse. So it is important to include healthy complex carbohydrates such as wholewheat bread and potatoes in your eating plan. Both starches and sugars raise blood sugar levels but processed sugar tends to give an instant "high" followed by a "low" and can actually make you feel hungry again within a very short time.

In the long run it is important to ease yourself away from sugar dependence, because of your figure, health, and teeth. (Dentists say that the best way to eat sweet things with least damage to your teeth is to eat them all at once, preferably with a meal, and then clean your teeth afterward.)

In the short term – and since this is a diet, you shouldn't keep it up for ever – here are ways of fitting in your longed-for extras and stopping yourself from going on a binge with frustration.

A lot of sugar in the diet causes the release of large quantities of insulin, whose job it is to reduce levels of sugar and fat in the blood by taking them out of the bloodstream and storing them in cells – helping you to accumulate body fat.

Eating smaller, more frequent meals seems to result in a more balanced insulin response and keeps blood sugar levels steady, which is thought to be better for slimmers.

This diet contains a healthy balance of foods but because some of the calories are in the form of snacks, the main meals have to be extra nutritious.

**Allowances:** Each day you are allowed 10 fl oz (275 ml) skimmed milk for tea and coffee, no sugar.

**Breakfasts:** Choose one a day.
1  4 portions fresh fruit, including 1 orange
2  1 egg, 1 slice wholewheat toast, 1 tsp butter
3  2 slices well-broiled bacon, 2 broiled tomatoes, 1 slice wholewheat bread
4  portion wholewheat cereal, 5 fl oz (150 ml) skimmed milk, 1 oz (25 g) raisins, 1 orange
5  portion wholewheat cereal, 5 fl oz (150 ml) skimmed milk, 1 apple, and orange juice
6  $\frac{3}{4}$ oz (20 g) bran flakes, 3 fl oz (75 ml) skimmed milk, $\frac{1}{2}$ oz (15 g) raisins or sultanas, $\frac{1}{2}$ oz (15 g) toasted almonds
7  1 medium-thick slice wholewheat toast, 1 tsp butter or margarine, 2 tsp honey or marmalade, 1 apple

**Main meals:** Choose two each day.
1  egg salad made with 1 hard-boiled egg and any combination of the following: cucumber, lettuce, radishes, celery or water-chestnuts
add 3 oz (75 g) lima beans or red kidney beans and 1 tbsp vinaigrette dressing
1 medium-thick slice wholewheat bread
1 satsuma or 2 oz (50 g) grapes
2  broccoli and ham cheese:
roll 2 cooked broccoli spears in 2 thin slices lean ham
pour on 4 tbsp white sauce and sprinkle with $\frac{1}{2}$ oz (15 g) grated cheddar cheese
broil to heat through and brown
serve with 2 broiled tomatoes and 2 oz (50 g) peas
3  3 oz (75 g) lean roast meat
1 tbsp gravy
large portion braised red cabbage
large portion brussels sprouts
3 oz (75 g) broad beans or navy beans
3 oz (75 g) boiled potato
4  3 oz (75 g) calf liver thinly sliced and fried with a little onion in $\frac{1}{2}$ oz (15 g) butter or margarine
add seasoning and lemon juice to the pan, sprinkle with chopped parsley
4 oz (110 g) mashed potato
large portion carrots and celery
large portion braised cabbage
5  2 calf kidneys, halved and casseroled with onion, tomato puree, stock, and 1 tbsp sherry
add 1 sliced cooked beef sausage
1 oz (25 g) raw weight brown rice, boiled
large portion spinach

6  4 oz (110 g) rump steak, beaten and cut into thin strips, sauteed with onion in $\frac{1}{2}$ oz (15 g) butter
stir in 1 tbsp horseradish sauce and seasoning
broccoli
carrots
7  3 oz (75 g) herring, broiled
2 tbsp mustard sauce
5 oz (150 g) mashed or boiled potato
large portion sliced green beans
8  6 oz (175 g) white fish, poached with onion and herbs
2 tbsp parsley sauce
mixture of sliced zucchini, 1 chopped tomato, and $\frac{1}{2}$ sliced onion, simmered
4 oz (110 g) boiled potato
9  1 pork or lamb chop, don't eat the fat, casseroled with onion; green cabbage, stock, and cider
3 oz (75 g) peas
large portion whole french beans
10  2 egg omelette filled with cooked vegetables and 1 oz (25 g) grated cheddar cheese
salad of sliced tomato, onion, and cucumber

Each day allow yourself *one* of these.
1  1$\frac{1}{2}$ oz (40 g) chocolate
2  3 fancy chocolates
3  3 toffees
4  individual mousse and 2 cookies
5  4 oz (110 g) roast potato
6  2 large glasses white or red wine
7  2 single spirits with low-calorie mixer
8  1 individual chocolate ice cream
9  4 oz (110 g) ice cream
10  1 medium slice any cake
11  6 oz (175 g) rice pudding
12  1 doughnut with jam and cream
13  2 oz (60 g) portion apple strudel
14  1 mince pie
15  2 crackers
16  2 wafer biscuits
17  1 can beer
18  1 bar chocolate
19  6 thin mints

*A nutritious diet that builds in sweet treats and drinks to satisfy your cravings.*

# The You Don't Have To Eat Meat Diet

**(1200 calories a day)**
Vegetarians are usually healthy, rarely overweight, and their way of eating generally includes lots of nutritious fruit and vegetables. However, *just* cutting out meat won't make you healthy and slim, unless you remember some of the new guidelines. Don't replace meat with lots of hard cheese because it is high fat and high calorie. You can get all the protein you need with fish, pulses, cereals, and some dairy foods, and these also provide all the nutrients meat contains.

Although animal protein contains all the nine essential amino acids for your health, vegetable protein is usually missing one or more – but you can balance it all out by combining vegetables with other kinds of vegetables, and other foods. For instance, the Mexican dish of corn tortillas and beans does that. Other combinations that work include: leafy vegetables with most grains and cereals; beans with sesame or wheat; peanuts with barley, bran, or corn.

Don't forget the value of good wholewheat bread – it contains 9 g of fiber and 9 g of protein, as well as 40 g of starch per 100 g, and is a rich source of B vitamins.

This particular diet is for those who do not wish to eat meat. It is not for Vegans who do not eat fish, eggs, milk, cheese, or other animal foods.

**Allowances:** Each day you are allowed 10 fl oz (275 ml) skimmed milk for tea and coffee. That is enough for about 7 cups. Also drink water and low-calorie drinks as often as you like.

**Breakfasts:** Use the same list as The Fill Up With Fiber Diet (page 36).

**Light meals:** Choose one each day.
**1 Salad**
choose one of the following:
3 sardines
3 oz (75 g) canned salmon
3 oz (75 g) tuna in brine
1 hard-boiled egg with 1 tbsp yogurt dressing
4 oz (110 g) cottage cheese
1 oz (25 g) hard cheese such as cheddar
with any 2 salads:
   chopped celery, cucumber, 4 oz (110 g) diced beetroot, chicory, and slices of orange
   onion, 2 oz (50 g) sweet corn, beans, 3 oz (75 g) lima beans, sliced mushrooms and low-fat natural yogurt
   grated carrot, 1 oz (25 g) raisins, and lemon juice
**2 Omelette**
2 eggs, seasoning, 2 tbsp milk (try a souffle omelette sometimes by separating the egg whites, whipping them, and folding into the yolk before cooking)
Fillings
1 oz (25 g) grated cheese and minced onion
3 oz (75 g) cooked sweet corn
4 oz (110 g) cooked spinach with ½ oz (15 g) chopped peanuts
3 oz (75 g) peeled shrimps
3 oz (75 g) peas and sliced poached mushrooms
with 1 medium-thick slice wholewheat bread
large portion broccoli, cabbage, or beans
**3 Open sandwich**
1 medium-thick slice wholewheat bread with 1 tsp butter or margarine, lettuce, and cucumber slices
Toppings
3 oz (75 g) peeled shrimps mixed with 1 tbsp yogurt dressing
2 oz (50 g) smoked or canned salmon with lemon slices
3 oz (75 g) canned tuna in brine and apple slices
3 oz (75 g) cottage cheese and pear slices
2 sardines and 2 slices beetroot
**4 White fish**
poach or grill 7 oz (200 g) cod, haddock, hake, skate or plaice
Accompaniments
very fine strips of carrot and celery cooked in ½ oz (15 g) butter
1 oz (25 g) wholewheat breadcrumbs, sliced mushrooms and grated onion mixed with 1 tbsp cream
3 tbsp parsley sauce

1 sliced zucchini, tomato and sliced onion, cooked in stock
½ oz (15 g) each of grated cheese and wholewheat breadcrumbs – broil to melt and brown
**5 Oily fish**
choose one of these:
7 oz (200 g) trout
5 oz (150 g) fresh herring
4 oz (110 g) mackerel fillet
Accompaniments
½ oz (15 g) toasted flaked almonds
3 tbsp mustard sauce
3 tbsp cucumber sauce
serve with 6 oz (175 g) plain boiled rice or baked potato and green salad
**6 Baked potato**
bake a 7 oz (200 g) potato, scoop out some of the flesh, and fill
return to the oven to heat filling through
Fillings
3 oz (75 g) sweet corn and 1 tbsp sour cream
3 oz (75 g) shrimps, chopped celery, and ½ oz (15 g) chopped walnuts
1 oz (25 g) grated cheese and 1 tbsp sweet pickle
3 oz (75 g) cooked white fish and 1 tbsp tartare sauce
3 oz (75 g) baked beans
2 oz (50 g) cottage cheese and 2 oz (50 g) sweet corn
dessert: portion of fresh fruit
**7 Pasta/rice**
2 oz (50 g) raw weight brown rice or wholewheat pasta, boiled, mixed with any one of these:
Accompaniments
1 hard-boiled egg, 2 tbsp curry sauce and 2 oz (50 g) peas
3 oz (75 g) cooked diced white fish, 1 oz (25 g) peas, 1 oz (25 g) butter beans and a chopped tomato
4 tbsp cheese sauce

**Main Meal 2:** Choose any of the meals indicated for Main Meal 1, and include any one of these starters.
**1** 10 fl oz (275 ml) clear soup
**2** 10 fl oz (275 ml) homemade vegetable soup
**3** ½ melon
**4** ½ large grapefruit topped with 1 tsp sugar and broiled
**5** segments from 1 small orange and 1 small grapefruit
**6** 5 fl oz (150 ml) tomato or orange or grapefruit juice
**7** ½ pear filled with 2 oz (50 g) cottage cheese on lettuce
**8** 1 hard-boiled egg, mix yolk with yogurt dressing and pipe back into whites
serve with tomato, lettuce

*A diet without meat needs to be well balanced to provide all the essential nutrients.*

# The Suit Your Moods Diet

(Strict Days: 800 calories; Normal Days: 1200 calories; Nibbling Days: 1100 calories)

There are good days, when being sensible about food seems easy, and other times when all you feel you want to do is eat and eat.

This diet allows you to be flexible, both about eating meals and nibbling bits and pieces. There are three basic levels of eating: Strict Days, when you have lots of will power; Normal Days, when you want to eat just three meals a day; and Nibbling Days, when you feel like eating more frequently.

Whatever the circumstances, these guidelines should help you cut the calories and lose weight. But aim to have as many Normal Days, where you have three meals a day, as possible. Try to have up to two Strict Days a week, no more; and one or two Nibbling Days at most.

**Allowances:** Each day you are allowed 10 fl oz (275 ml) skimmed milk for tea and coffee, no sugar. Also plenty of low-calorie drinks and water.

**Breakfasts:** Choose one of these:
1 3 heaped tbsp bran cereal or portion wholewheat cereal
2 3 pieces fresh fruit
3 1 slice wholewheat bread
1 tsp butter or margarine
1 tsp honey
1 piece fresh fruit

## STRICT DAYS
**Main Meal 1:** Choose one each day.
1 1 apple and 1 banana
4 oz (110 g) cottage cheese
2 huge salad of lettuce, cucumber, celery, 1 oz (25 g) raisins, ½ diced apple, 1 oz (25 g) diced cheddar cheese
1 tbsp yogurt dressing
3 fruit salad made from:
1 orange, 1 slice pineapple, 1 kiwi fruit, 1 apple, 1 grapefruit
4 ½ melon, 10 cherries
5 dates or 3 dried figs
5 5 oz (150 g) low-fat natural yogurt
1 oz (25 g) raisins
1 apple or pear

**Main Meal 2:** Choose one each day.
1 1 egg, boiled, poached, or scrambled
1 slice wholewheat bread
either 3 oz (75 g) peas
or 1 portion fresh fruit
2 4 oz (110 g) white fish, broiled or poached

large portions of 2 green vegetables such as green cabbage, broccoli, sliced green beans, spinach, spring greens
3 10 fl oz (275 ml) any low-calorie soup
2 slices wholewheat bread
2 fresh apricots or plums or 1 satsuma
4 5 oz (150 g) cottage cheese on lettuce surrounded by lots of fresh fruit
5 8 oz (225 g) chicken joint, no skin, casseroled with carrots and onions green beans or mashed turnip and 3 oz (75 g) peas or broad beans

## NORMAL DAYS – when you feel like eating three meals
**Main Meal 1:** Choose one a day, variations are given in italics.
1 2 frozen fish cakes
2 broiled tomatoes
2 oz (50 g) peas
2 oz (50 g) sweet corn
1 large apple
*omit sweet corn and add 1 tbsp tartare sauce and lots of sliced green beans*
2 3½ oz (100 g) cod steak with 3 oz (75 g) white sauce
4 oz (110 g) mashed potato
large portion poached mushrooms
1 large orange
*add to the sauce either: 2 oz (50 g) peeled shrimps or ½ oz (15 g) grated cheese; omit potato and add 1 oz (25 g) raw weight brown rice*
3 3 oz (75 g) any lean roast meat
1 tbsp gravy
3 oz (75 g) roast potato
large portion braised red cabbage
broccoli
*make meat into kebabs before cooking; substitute apple, cranberry, or horseradish sauce for gravy*
4 4 oz (110 g) chicken breast baked in foil with onion, mushrooms, and mixed herbs
2 tbsp white sauce
large portion green beans
large portion sliced carrots
*use 8 oz (225 g) chicken portion without skin, instead of chicken breast; use any other green vegetable instead of green beans*
5 2 oz (50 g) burger, broiled, with 2 oz (50 g) bun and
1 tbsp relish
1 sliced tomato
1 portion fresh fruit
*use 1 large sausage instead of burger*
6 5 oz (150 g) can baked beans
1 slice wholewheat toast
1 tsp butter
1 poached egg
*replace toast and butter with 1 oz (25 g) grated cheese on baked beans*
7 10 fl oz (275 ml) can any low-calorie soup

2 crispbreads
4 oz (110 g) cottage cheese
2 portions fresh fruit
*replace crispbreads by ½ slice bread; replace cottage cheese with 1 oz (25 g) hard cheese or 1 hard-boiled egg*

**Main Meal 2:** Follow the guidelines for Main Meal 1 and add any one of these to each meal.
1 4 oz (110 g) boiled or baked potato
2 1 oz (25 g) cheddar cheese
3 1 large glass red or white wine
4 1 oz (25 g) raw weight brown rice or pasta
5 individual tub low-fat natural yogurt and 1 orange
6 10 fl oz (275 ml) can any low-calorie soup
7 1 oz (25 g) pâté and 1 crispbread and salad
8 ½ grapefruit and 1 tsp sugar

## NIBBLING DAYS – when you want to eat all the time.
Make a huge pot of vegetable soup from stock, turnip, cabbage, parsnip, onion, leeks, tomato puree, and seasoning

During the day, eat 10 of the following, and try to eat at least 6 different foods.
1 10 fl oz (275 ml) vegetable soup
2 1 large orange and 1 large apple
3 1 very large banana
4 1½ oz (40 g) raisins or sultanas
5 ¾ oz (20 g) nuts
6 1 oz (25 g) cheddar cheese
7 portion wholewheat cereal
8 2 squares chocolate
9 individual tub frozen mousse
10 1 boiled or poached egg
11 2 beef sausages, well broiled
12 2 oz (50 g) lean cooked meat
13 4 oz (110 g) poached or broiled white fish
14 large portion any leafy vegetable and 2 oz (50 g) peas
15 3 oz (75 g) sweet corn
16 2 oz (50 g) canned salmon
17 1 oz (25 g) raw weight pasta or rice, boiled
18 10 prunes
19 4 oz (110 g) peeled shrimps
20 2 cookies
21 2 crispbreads and 1 tsp butter
22 4 oz (110 g) cottage cheese
23 5 oz (150 g) tub low-fat natural yogurt and 1 piece fruit
24 2 broiled fish sticks
Plus unlimited lettuce, cucumber, raw carrots and low-calorie drinks.

*A flexible diet to suit your mood and changing life-style.*

# The Fifteen Hundred Diet

Many experts now believe that it is possible to slim down with a plan that gives a greater number of calories than most diets have traditionally allowed. And you will be less likely to put back the surplus pounds because you will have had longer to fashion yourself a better life-style.

This diet is suitable for any woman who has more than 28 lb (13 kg) to lose, for active men, and for children. The generous helpings allow you to feel satisfied while still cutting calories. But because this is a slow diet, it will give you the chance to retrain your tastebuds. As it allows up to 1500 calories a day, there is absolutely no room for cheating. Watch your portions. Keep your weighing scales handy and use kitchen measure spoons.

Some extremely overweight people can lose weight on as much as 1700 calories a day. However, if you do find that the surplus fat just does not shift on a higher-calorie diet, then reduce your calorie intake slightly, but only after about two to three weeks of no results – and *do* increase your activities. You cannot expect a diet to give permanent and satisfactory results all by itself, without building in exercise.

**Allowances:** Each day you are allowed up to 10 fl oz (275 ml) skimmed milk for tea and coffee, no sugar. Also plenty of water and low-calorie drinks.

**Breakfasts:** Choose one each day.

**1** 1 egg, poached or boiled
1 medium-thick slice wholewheat toast
1 tsp butter or margarine
2 slices bacon, well-broiled
**2** 2 eggs, scrambled (no fat)
2 medium-thick slices wholewheat toast
**3** 3 oz (75 g) kipper fillets
2 broiled tomatoes
1 medium-thick slice wholewheat bread
**4** 5 heaped tbsp bran cereal
5 fl oz (150 ml) skimmed milk
1 small chopped apple, 2 chopped apricots
**5** portion wholewheat cereal
1 tbsp raisins or sultanas
5 fl oz (150 ml) skimmed milk
**6** 5 tbsp muesli
5 fl oz (150 ml) skimmed milk
or low-fat natural yogurt
**7** portion wholewheat cereal
2 tbsp chopped dried fruit
5 fl oz (150 ml) skimmed milk

**Main meals:** Choose two each day.

**1** 7 oz (200 g) baked potato
1 oz (25 g) grated cheddar cheese
5 oz (150 g) can baked beans
**2** 4 oz (110 g) broiled burger
2 oz (50 g) burger bun
sliced tomato, cucumber, and gherkin
**3** 1 oz (25 g) liver pâté
1 medium-thick slice wholewheat bread
salad of lettuce, cucumber, and tomato
**4** 8 oz (225 g) chicken joint, skin removed, baked in foil with onion and seasoning
large portions of sliced beans and spinach or spring greens
large portion raspberries with 2 tbsp cream
**5** 3 broiled fish sticks
3 oz (75 g) french fries
2 oz (50 g) peas
1 apple or small banana or peach
**6** ½ large grapefruit
3 oz (75 g) lean roast meat
2 tbsp gravy
4 oz (110 g) roast potato
large portion mixed peas and carrots
**7** 5 fl oz (150 ml) tomato or vegetable or grapefruit juice
6 oz (175 g) white fish fillet, broiled without fat, garnished with 8 green grapes
2 oz (50 g) peas with chopped onion
1 glass white wine
2 oz (50 g) ice cream or sherbert
**8** 5 oz (150 g) broiled trout
½ oz (15 g) toasted almonds and lemon wedge

2 broiled tomatoes
large portion poached mushrooms
1 glass red wine
1 oz (25 g) cheddar or other hard cheese
celery sticks
**9** 5 fl oz (150 ml) grapefruit juice
lamb kebab made with 4 oz (110 g) lean diced lamb
1 oz (25 g) raw weight brown rice, boiled and mixed with 2 oz (50 g) peas and ½ oz (15 g) pistachio nuts
large portion whole green beans
**10** toasted cheese made with
2 medium-thick slices wholewheat bread
2 oz (50 g) grated cheddar cheese mixed with 2 tbsp skimmed milk and dash Worcestershire sauce, topped with tomato slices
**11** 4 oz (110 g) minute steak, broiled and topped with 1 oz (25 g) pâté
braised celery
2 broiled tomatoes
½ oz (15 g) potato chips
**12** 2 large "beef" tomatoes, filled with 4 oz (110 g) savoury mince and baked serve each on ½ medium-thick slice toast
2 oz (50 g) sweet corn
1 large orange or other fresh fruit
**13** 1 baked egg
3 oz (75 g) cooked chicken meat with 3 tbsp curry sauce
1 oz (25 g) raw weight brown rice, boiled
cucumber slices in natural yogurt
**14** 4 oz (110 g) calf liver, broiled
2 slices well-broiled bacon
2 broiled tomatoes
6 oz (175 g) baked potato
large portion poached mushrooms
1 portion fresh fruit

*A long-term diet that will allow you to change your eating habits and lose weight gradually, without starving.*

# Slimming and Your Life-style

You can be overweight at any age, from childhood to old age, and each part of our lives bring different temptations and problems.

School lunches are often stodgy, while café choices with strong emphasis on hamburgers, french fries, and pies, competing with less-than-appetizing cold, limp salads, are also a danger. An attractively presented packed lunch is a better alternative.

Snack time is a problem for school children, just home and very hungry. Sitting watching television munching a carrot is not going to satisfy the urge for carbohydrates. A huge snack followed by a big supper piles on the calories. One way out? Divide a day's reasonable amount of food into five smallish meals: breakfast, lunch, snack, main evening meal, and a small snack before bedtime. Plan ahead and remember high-fiber foods are more filling.

When you go out to work you often eat out in cafés or restaurants. When choosing from a menu, try to stick to thin soups, melon, or grapefruit for starters. Avoid potted meats or shrimps, pâté, anything with pastry, or fried food. For a main course, try to steer your way round the rich, fatty dishes — avoid anything with cheese, butter, or cream.

Mothers at home have the opportunity to snack, and when you're cooking it's all too easy to have a taster. Try not to eat snacks with the children or finish up leftovers. Write yourself out a daily plan — and stick to it.

When you're older, your energy needs are less, but you still need nutritious food, so try not to fill up on cakes, cookies, or bread and jam. Be sure to eat fresh fruit and vegetables, and watch your calcium intake because of the risk of osteoporosis (thinning of the bones). Drink skimmed low-fat milk and consider calcium supplements.

## HOW TO CHANGE YOUR LIFE-STYLE – for the better

If you have a weight problem, dieting isn't enough: you also need to modify your habits. Psychologists call it "behavior therapy" or "behavior modification."

Your first step is to note what you eat — and when. Write yourself a detailed diet diary. Keeping records helps you to realize what you are doing. Where do you eat your meals? When do you eat? How often? How long did the meal take? Your records may well reveal certain recurring patterns of behavior associated with eating. You may notice, for instance, that you always feel hungry at a certain time of the day, but not always at mealtimes.

### Making changes

● Do you eat sweets while you are driving? Stop buying them.
● Feel like a snack when watching television? Try keeping your hands occupied, with knitting or sewing.
● Feel hungry in the afternoon? Go out for a walk.
● Do you always want to eat after having an argument at home? Decide to do 8 to 12 repetitions of

an exercise instead.

● Are you always rushing around with no time to sit down and eat? Only eat when you do it properly, sitting down, with a knife and fork. Never eat on the run.

## Ploys

● Make snacking more inconvenient to do. If you want a slice of bread, for example, take out just one piece, wrap up the loaf and put it away. Toast the bread.

● Use smaller dishes so your plate looks full with smaller portions.

● Eat slowly. Cut your food into smaller pieces and chew for longer. Place cutlery back on the table between every two or three bites, and have a restful pause now and again between mouthfuls. The slower you eat, the quicker you will feel full – on less food.

● Drink a glass of acidic juice such as grapefruit, lime juice, or unsweetened lemonade (home-made) twenty minutes before a meal to reduce your appetite. Researchers say that it takes about twenty minutes to feel full after you start eating because that is the time it takes for a hormone called cholecystokinin (CCK) to be re-leased in the small intestine. Liquids such as juice or even tea or coffee stimulate the release of CCK secretion and send the brain a message of fullness *before* you eat.

## Activity

Feel that you *do* run around a lot? Get yourself a pedometer, a small precision instrument calibrated to your stride length and operated by an internal pendulum that registers each step. Record your total mileage for a week, day by day.

In tests, the average distance walked by overweight women was about 41 percent less than that walked by slim women. Fat men walked an average of 39 percent less than slim men. So encourage yourself to be more active.

You need to experience enjoyment and success to keep up the relearning process, or you can easily become discouraged. Activity will become more fun if you plan it carefully, and goals get realistic.

First step: as you did with food, write down your daily pattern of physical activity, including sleeping, eating, bathing, and working. Divide this into light exercise, moderate, and heavy. Then replace your sedentary activities with more vigorous ones. For example . . .

## Walk

● If you drive to work, park about half a mile away and walk. Brisk walking, to and from your car, twice a day, five days a week, could well burn up about 7 lb (3 kg) of fat in a year. But more important, it is having an effect on your health and helping to ginger up your metabolism.

● If you take a bus, get off at an earlier bus stop and walk the rest of the way.

● Put the alarm clock on earlier and take a brisk walk before breakfast.

● Take a twenty-minute walk instead of an early evening drink.

● Walk up and down the stairs at work if it is possible. Get up and walk after some hours of work, instead of having a snack.

## Reward Yourself

Keep a chart to record your progress. Provide yourself with goals — for instance, a certain amount of exercise, so many miles or landmarks to pass. Every time you achieve it, put some money in a bottle. Eventually, buy yourself something that helps to make activity more of a pleasure.

# GET YOURSELF FIT

**Condition your body, relax with yoga or shake a leg with jazz dancing . . . and there are a lot more exercise classes to choose from, so select something to suit you. Here are the most popular regimes for you to try.**

The image of physical exercise as punishment is fast dying off. Today, the joy of sport and the fun of exercise are part of a whole new cult of healthy living.

Besides the health and body benefits, exercise can also produce feelings of well-being, reducing depression and helping us to deal with the increased stresses of living, especially in cities.

Evidence suggests that when exercise is vigorous, like running, it stimulates the body's natural mood-influencing compounds (pain-killers, similar to morphine) which could explain "the high."

Research by the British Heart Foundation suggests that while adrenaline, the "fight or flight" hormone, is produced by negative, passive emotions like anxiety and uncertainty, noradrenaline — its partner hormone which is part of the body's sympathetic nervous system — is a response to more active emotions like competition, anger, and aggression.

Physical exercise triggers noradrenaline, which in turn stimulates the pleasure centers of the brain both during activity and for a while afterward.

Exercise isn't easy if you are overweight. You will probably not be very mobile and it will take quite a bit of effort to start. In addition, you may well feel self-conscious about your size in public.

Fat makes you move slowly and moving slowly seems to make you stay fat.

But if you have the kind of metabolism that is so efficient at laying down fat that you almost have to starve to lose surplus pounds, then cutting down food drastically may make your metabolism even slower. It is self-defeating.

The only way to speed it up, say many experts, is to break the vicious circle with a sensible, nutritious long-term eating plan *plus* consistent, regular exercise. Keep it gentle to begin with. And do check with your doctor first.

For encouragement, why not join a class? If you are worried about your size, try an exercise group attached to a slimming club. There will be people there in the same boat, and you won't feel different.

Always do *warm-ups* to gradually boost the supply of oxygen to your muscles. When you finish exercising, be sure to *cool down* with gentler exercises. This gradually tails off the more vigorous movements, reducing the likelihood of getting an uneven heartbeat. If you stop exercising suddenly, you could cause pooling of the blood in the legs, which decreases the return of blood to the heart.

For that reason, too, do not have a sauna or hot shower immediately after exercise. High temperatures increase the heart rate and smoking can also cause an irregular heartbeat.

Exercise to music, it's much more fun; both at home and in class. Practicing your movements in front of a mirror helps you get the right body line.

Don't wear anything too tight or restricting (jeans are a bad idea). A loose tracksuit or easy leotard and tights are more comfortable.

Exercise is not just for the young. Older people who take it up can add weight and strength to their bones, while building and maintaining muscle. It is the *real* secret of staying younger.

# Test your Fitness

> **Note: Do not undertake any of the following tests and exercises if you are very overweight, or have a history of illness or back trouble, without first checking with your doctor.**

## STAMINA ... how long can you last out?

### THE STEP TEST
This test was first devised by Harvard University during the World War II, and involves stepping up on to a stool, bench, or the stairs (preferably about 16 inches (40 cm) high) and down again for a period of 3 minutes. Step up with one foot, bring up the other, then step down again, one after the other, repeating the sequence in a steady rhythm about 24 times per minute (men) and 21 times per minute (women).

After 3 minutes of "step ups," remain standing and count your pulse over 15 seconds, beginning your count 5 seconds after the completion of the tests. The lower your heart rate over the 15 seconds, the better your physical condition.

### Number of heartbeats counted in 15 seconds ... and your rating

#### WOMEN
| Under 45 | Over 45 | Fitness rating |
|---|---|---|
| Below 20 | Below 21 | EXCELLENT |
| 20–22 | 21–23 | GOOD |
| 23–28 | 24–29 | AVERAGE |
| Above 28 | Above 29 | POOR |

#### MEN
| Under 45 | Over 45 | Fitness rating |
|---|---|---|
| Below 18 | Below 19 | EXCELLENT |
| 18–20 | 19–21 | GOOD |
| 21–25 | 22–26 | AVERAGE |
| Above 25 | Above 26 | POOR |

### SIMPLE STAMINA TESTS
**1** Walk steadily, without stopping, up three flights of stairs (try it the next time you go to a big store and don't take the elevator). Each flight should comprise about 15 to 20 steps. Can you climb and still carry on a normal conversation? **Fit**
Are you so breathless when you reach the top you cannot talk without panting? **Average**
Are you too breathless to continue after only one flight? **Unfit**
**2** Can you run for a bus – say a distance of about 50 yards (45 m) – without gasping for breath? **Fit**
Or do you wheeze and gasp? **Unfit**
**3** Run on the spot lifting your feet at least 6 inches (15 cm) off the ground. If you are over 50, you should manage 2 minutes comfortably. Younger people should find 3 minutes easy. If you are fit, of course!
**4** Try this running test only if you are fit enough to do the step test without problems. Jog for a mile. You should be able to talk comfortably without being too breathless during and after the test if you are really fit.

**If the run takes....**
**More than 20 minutes** You are very sedentary
**15–20 minutes** You are inactive
**Less than 15 minutes** You are moderately active
**10–12 minutes** You are an active person – probably you go jogging
**Less than 10 minutes** You sound like an athlete
As a simple rule of thumb, if you are under 45, you are fit if you can do it in about 10 minutes. Over 45? Add a minute for every 5 years. Women should add 2 minutes in each age group.

## SUPPLENESS ... how flexible are you?

**1** Stand with legs together and try to clasp your hands behind your back, with one hand over your shoulder. (Repeat on the other side.) If you can do a full handclasp, score 2 points. Fingers touching: 1 point. Fingers cannot touch at all: 0 points.

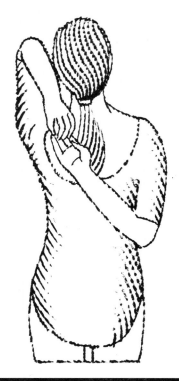

## STRENGTH TEST

Lie face down on the floor, elbows bent, hands resting on the floor. Now do push-ups. Extend your arms and push yourself up off the floor, keeping the body in a straight line. Lower gently back. Do this as many times as possible in 2 minutes. But *don't* push yourself to do more than you can – be honest.

| FEMALE | Age | Excellent | Good | Average | Fair | Poor |
|---|---|---|---|---|---|---|
| | 20–29 | 49+ | 34–48 | 17–33 | 6–16 | 0–5 |
| | 30–39 | 40+ | 25–39 | 12–24 | 4–11 | 0–3 |
| | 40–49 | 35+ | 20–34 | 8–19 | 3–7 | 0–2 |
| | 50–59 | 30+ | 15–29 | 6–14 | 2–5 | 0–1 |
| | 60–69 | 20+ | 5–19 | 3–4 | 1–2 | 0 |
| **MALE** | **Age** | **Excellent** | **Good** | **Average** | **Fair** | **Poor** |
| | 20–29 | 55+ | 45–54 | 35–44 | 20–34 | 0–19 |
| | 30–39 | 45+ | 35–44 | 25–34 | 15–24 | 0–14 |
| | 40–49 | 40+ | 30–39 | 20–29 | 12–19 | 0–11 |
| | 50–59 | 35+ | 25–34 | 15–24 | 8–14 | 0–7 |
| | 60–69 | 30+ | 20–29 | 10–19 | 5–9 | 0–4 |

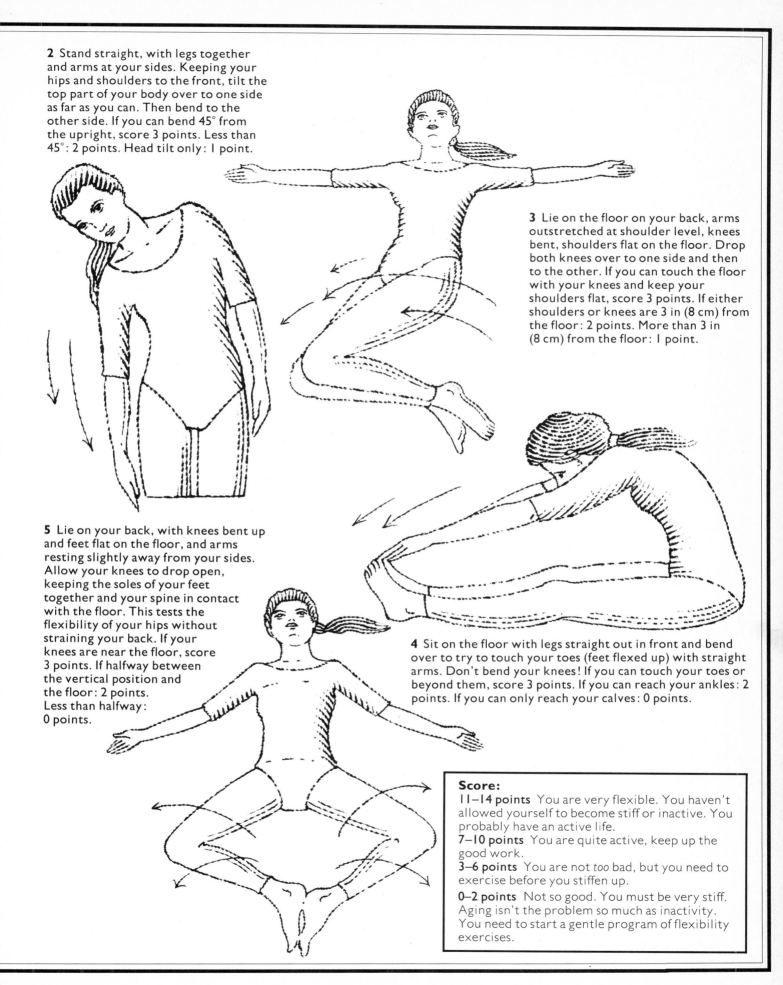

**2** Stand straight, with legs together and arms at your sides. Keeping your hips and shoulders to the front, tilt the top part of your body over to one side as far as you can. Then bend to the other side. If you can bend 45° from the upright, score 3 points. Less than 45°: 2 points. Head tilt only: I point.

**3** Lie on the floor on your back, arms outstretched at shoulder level, knees bent, shoulders flat on the floor. Drop both knees over to one side and then to the other. If you can touch the floor with your knees and keep your shoulders flat, score 3 points. If either shoulders or knees are 3 in (8 cm) from the floor: 2 points. More than 3 in (8 cm) from the floor: I point.

**5** Lie on your back, with knees bent up and feet flat on the floor, and arms resting slightly away from your sides. Allow your knees to drop open, keeping the soles of your feet together and your spine in contact with the floor. This tests the flexibility of your hips without straining your back. If your knees are near the floor, score 3 points. If halfway between the vertical position and the floor: 2 points. Less than halfway: 0 points.

**4** Sit on the floor with legs straight out in front and bend over to try to touch your toes (feet flexed up) with straight arms. Don't bend your knees! If you can touch your toes or beyond them, score 3 points. If you can reach your ankles: 2 points. If you can only reach your calves: 0 points.

**Score:**
**11–14 points** You are very flexible. You haven't allowed yourself to become stiff or inactive. You probably have an active life.
**7–10 points** You are quite active, keep up the good work.
**3–6 points** You are not *too* bad, but you need to exercise before you stiffen up.
**0–2 points** Not so good. You must be very stiff. Aging isn't the problem so much as inactivity. You need to start a gentle program of flexibility exercises.

# Posture Improvement and Relaxation

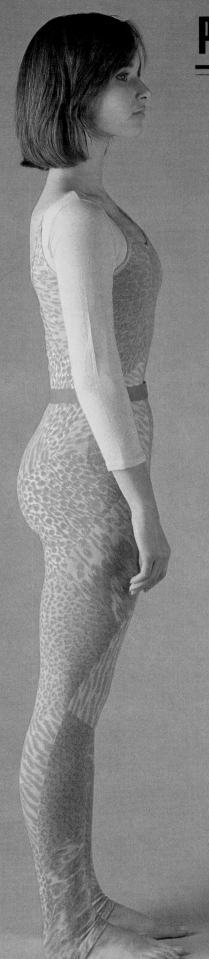

The way you stand, sit, and walk is all to do with your posture. Good posture can make you appear to lose pounds in seconds and it certainly helps you to look younger. Bad posture encourages stiffness and muscle tension and can lead to back problems. If you stoop and slouch you give a less positive, less confident image of yourself to the world. It is "body language" working against you! But you can straighten yourself out with conscious concentration and exercise. First assess your own posture. Does your stomach stick out? Have you got a sway back? Do you stoop with bent shoulders and shuffle when you walk? This kind of posture can make you look older, fatter and, even shorter.

## Check list

Stand with your legs slightly apart, your weight evenly balanced on the balls of your feet. Lengthen the back of your neck and imagine you are being pulled upward from the top of your head as if you were suspended on a string. Keep your shoulders down but not stiff. Your chin should be at a right angle to your throat. Flatten your stomach and tuck in your buttocks. Stretch your spine. Your ribcage should be down and your arms hanging loosely at your sides. *That* is good posture. If you were to draw a straight line through a drawing of your body, it should go through the ear, shoulder, knee, and front of the ankle.

When you walk, look straight ahead and do not stare at the ground. Keep your heel height to no more than 2 inches (4 cm). If you wear very high heels it throws the body out of alignment, tilting the pelvis and putting a strain on the lower back. The chain reaction will affect every part of your body.

Tight jeans also put a strain on the lower back. They compress your flesh and cause pressure. Don't wear halter necks because the dragging effect can give you back, neck, and shoulder ache. When shopping, divide your purchases into bags of equal weight for better balance, rather than carrying one

extra heavy bag. When lifting, don't bend from the waist, but bend your knees and lift the object close to your body, putting the strain on the thigh muscles, not your back. When gardening, don't bend over, kneel down – the same goes for scrubbing the floor. Protect your knees with a rubber pad or mat.

## Relaxation methods

Autogenic Therapy is a technique for learning relaxation and concentration. It is a way of talking to your body. Try lying back in an armchair or a flat cushioned surface such as a carpet, and imagine that your limbs are beginning to feel warm and heavy. Say to yourself out loud "My left arm is heavy," "My shoulders are heavy" – all parts of the body should be included.

Meditation is another way of achieving relaxation – it is the non-exercise side of yoga and is intended to calm the body and mind and distract the attention away from worries. Focus on a single object such as a candle flame or even a flower or picture, and concentrate on repeating a single word or phrase. Any word will do: it's a matter of personal choice. (But research on the effects of meditation and blood pressure have shown good results, it is claimed, when the word "one" was used.) As with other methods of relaxation, adopt a comfortable position and relax each part of the body in turn from top to toe. Once you feel at ease, concentrate on breathing slowly and naturally, repeating your key word as you exhale, for about 10 minutes at a stretch. It would be better not to meditate on a full stomach because you might fall asleep and the idea is to have some control over your conscious body.

Regular repeated movements of the body in the form of any gentle rhythmic exercise can also be very relaxing and has been found to lower blood pressure. Concentrating your mind and body totally in this way helps to blot out problems and provides an outlet for bottled-up feelings.

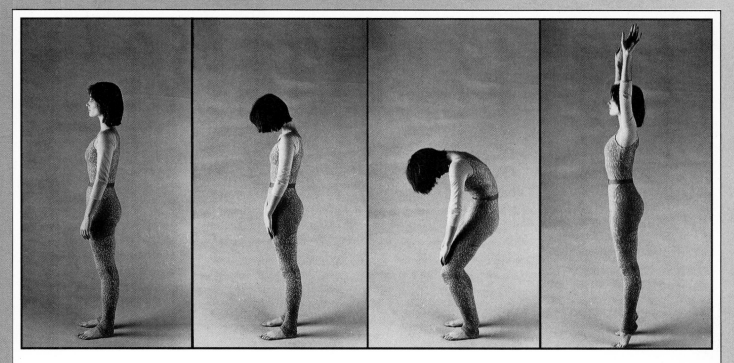

## POSTURE EXERCISE

Stand with your feet slightly apart, arms relaxed and by your sides, shoulders relaxed, head up. Drop your chin on to your chest and slowly bend forwards, letting your arms and hands droop and bending your knees. Pull in your stomach. Slowly straighten your legs and uncurl again. Reach up with your arms above your head and stretch up on to your toes. Relax. Repeat 3 times.

## POSITIVE REST

Try this mental and physical exercise whenever you need to relax, stop tension, and make yourself more serene. Preferably, do it before you go to bed or *before* your evening meal. Stay in position for about 20 minutes ideally, but 45 minutes maximum.

1 Lie flat on your back. A thickly carpeted floor would be suitable but do not lie on your bed – it is too soft and springy. If the floor seems hard, lie on a folded blanket or towel. Put a small pillow under your head.

2 Bend your knees and space feet about hip-width apart with the feet flat on the floor, toes pointing forward. Your pelvis should be flat and try to press the center of your back flat to the floor, pulling in your tummy. You want to avoid an arched back. Relax your shoulders, keep your neck close to the floor and raise your arms to the ceiling before folding them across your chest. Do not tense your muscles but just rest your arms lightly over your body. *Check* that your knees are not opening outward or pressing inward.

3 Now comes the *letting go* part of the exercise. Pretend you are a floppy rag doll. In order to relax your muscles you need to learn to recognize muscle tension – you can be tense without realizing it.

Each muscle needs to be tensed or clenched, then you let go. So, starting at your toes, tense them up really hard, hold, then relax. Work up to your ankles, calves, knees, thighs, the pelvic area, and buttocks, the stomach, hands, arms, shoulders and chest, neck, and face.

4 Concentrate on each part of the body as you relax it. Try to clear all other thoughts and worries from your mind and just think "ankle," "stomach," "arm," and so on. If somebody should come round and lift your arm, after all this, it should be floppy like a rag doll. Nothing should be stiff.

# The Warm Up

Warming up your body increases circulation, helps to stretch your joints and muscles, and makes your body more receptive for harder exercise to come. Dancers need to warm up before they begin exercising so that muscles do not get torn or ligaments damaged. Although you will probably not be attempting anything quite so vigorous, you need the same kind of warm-up-and-stretch routine. You'll find it easier to keep a rhythm (and more fun) if you exercise to music.

## SHOULDER HUNCHES

Lift your left shoulder up toward your left ear. Lower your left shoulder and lift your right shoulder up to your right ear. Hunch your shoulders alternately 2 or 3 times.

## WAIST CIRCLES

Stand with your legs apart, hands on hips. Bend forward from the waist and circle around to the right, then to the back, to the left and forward again, in a continuous movement. Do 4, alternating the direction.

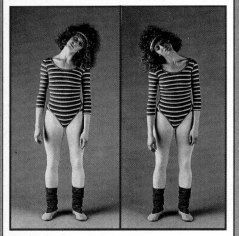

## HEAD ROLLS

Stand with your feet about shoulder-width apart, arms at your sides. Pull yourself up straight, tightening your stomach and buttock muscles. Drop your head forward with your chin sunk on your chest. Then roll your head around to the right, feeling the stretch on the left side of the neck. Straighten your neck to the upright position, drop your head over to the left, and roll it forward.

Repeat in the opposite direction and then do one more each way. Do not hunch your shoulders.

## SIDE STRETCHES

Standing with feet apart, lift your arms and stretch them above your head. Reach up to the ceiling with one arm, then reach up with the other arm. Do 10 stretches, alternating arms.

## BACK ROLL

Stand with feet wide apart, flop forward to touch your toes, hanging your head and arms down loosely like a rag doll. Then slowly unwind, vertebra by vertebra, until you stand straight again. Do this twice.

## WAIST BOUNCES

Standing with legs apart, stretch your right arm up and over your head to the left, stretching your waist. Stay there and bounce in gentle movements for a count of 4. Then reach up and over with the left arm and bounce to the right. Keep your shoulders back and don't bend forward.

## ARM SWINGS

Stand with feet apart, arms outstretched in front, knees bent. Then, bending over, swing your arms down through your legs and return to a half-way position. Swing through your legs again, stretching as far as you can. Stand up straight and repeat 8 times.

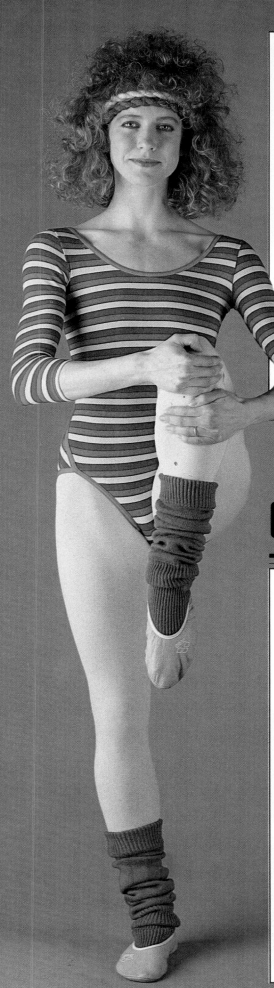

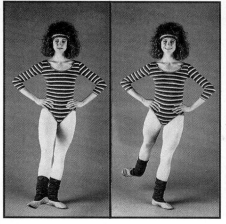

## LEG STRETCHES

Stand up straight, hands on hips, raise leg a few inches off the floor in front of you (keeping it straight) and circle your ankle. Rotate 4 times clockwise and 4 times anti-clockwise. Lower. Stretch the same leg out to the side and repeat the ankle rotations, then to the back. Change to the other leg and repeat.

## KNEE PULLS

Stand up straight, with your hands on your hips, and swing your right leg back. Then bring it forward, swinging it up in front of you and bending your knee. Grasp the knee with your hands and pull it up toward your body. Hold for a count of 4.

Release and repeat 4 times. Then repeat with the other leg. Shake out the legs to relax them.

# Cooling Down

1 Lie on the floor on your back and bend your knees up toward your chest. Hold them in and rock gently back and forward, relaxing your neck.
2 The yoga Plough exercise is ideal for "cooling down" the muscles after an exercise routine.

Lie on your back, raise your knees and straighten both legs into a vertical position. Continue the movement on so that your feet go over your head and your back lifts off the ground. Supporting your back with your hands, straighten your legs and take them right over your head. Try and touch the floor with your toes. Hold for as long as is comfortable and then carefully uncurl.

**1**

**2**

# California Stretch

The California Stretch is a system of stretching exercises – more vigorous than yoga, but gentler than aerobics. It is not so much good for heart-and-lung conditioning perhaps, but excellent for keeping you flexible and relaxed. Aerobics is nonstop, continuous exercise, pulse-raising and exhausting. California Stretch still makes you work, but not so furiously.

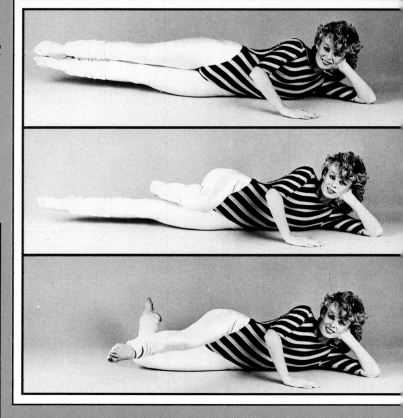

### SPINE STRAIGHTENER
Lie on your back on the floor, with your knees bent up, arms by your sides. Try to push your spine flat against the floor. Relax. Repeat 4 or 5 times.

### HEAD CIRCLES
Sit cross-legged on the floor, with a straight back, and do some head rolls. Drop your chin forward on to your chest, then slowly roll your head around to the left shoulder. Then roll it on around to the right – and back to the front. Do 2 rolls in each direction.

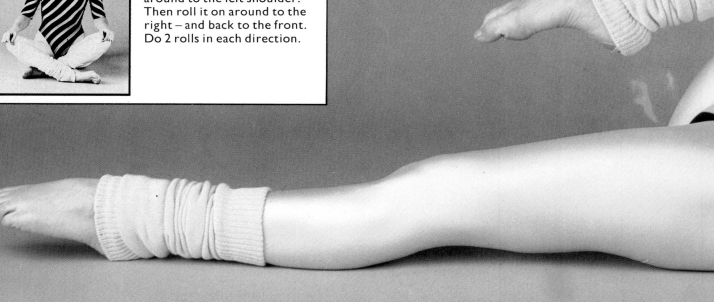

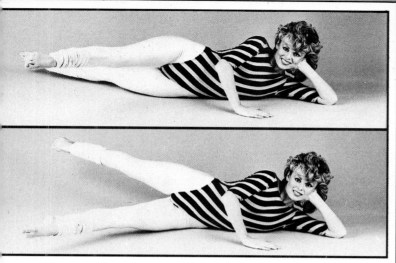

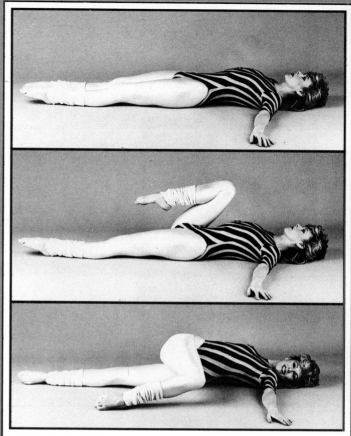

## SIDE CYCLES AND SCISSORS

Lie on your side on the floor, resting on your elbow, with the other hand palm-down on the floor in front of you, legs and body straight.

Raise both legs off the floor, about 3 inches (8 cm), and pedal as though riding a bike for a count of 5.

Still keeping your legs just off the floor (and straight) scissor them alternatvely backward and forward for 5 counts. Repeat these exercises 4 or 5 times each. Change sides and repeat.

## LEG CROSSES

Lie flat on your back on the floor, arms outstretched to the sides at shoulder level, legs straight.

Bend the right knee up, lift it to the chest, then drop it over the left leg on to the floor.

Repeat on the other side, and do this several times more with each leg.

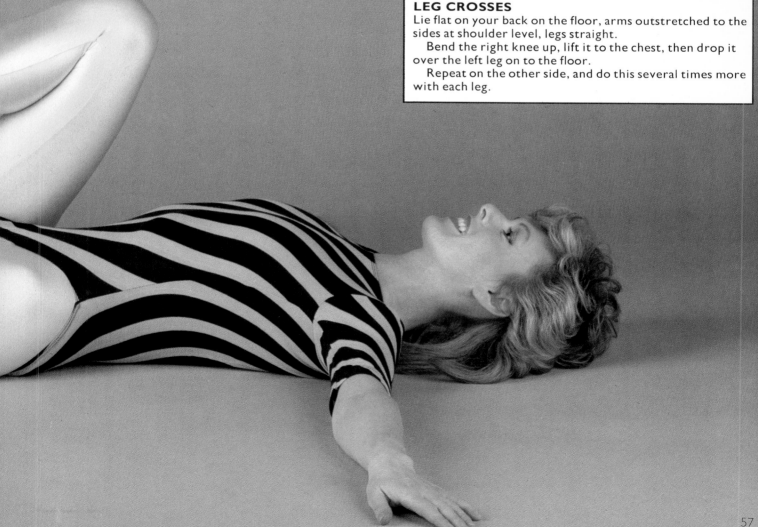

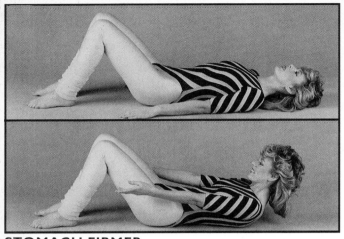

## STOMACH FIRMER

Lie on your back on the floor, with legs straight and arms by your sides. Press the base of your spine into the ground, bend your knees up, and lift your shoulders, pulling in your stomach muscles.

Hold for a count of 3, then relax by rolling down, vertebra by vertebra, until you are lying flat on the floor again. Make your stomach muscles do the work.

## BEND OVERS

Stand with legs apart, arms stretched high above your head, fingers interlocking. Tuck your stomach and bottom in. Knees should be slightly bent.

Lean over and touch your right foot with both hands (bend your knees farther if necessary). Straighten up and return to the first position.

Then lean down and touch your left foot. Repeat 8 to 10 times in alternate directions.

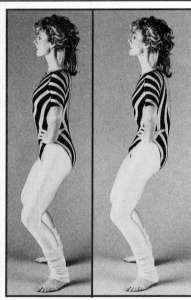

## PELVIC PUSHES

Stand, knees bent with your feet slightly apart and toes turned out, hands resting on hips. Tuck your buttocks under, and pull in your stomach. Push your hips forward, clenching your buttock muscles. Then swing buttocks back and relax.

Stand with knees and feet together, knees still slightly bent, and push your hips forward, tightening the buttocks. Relax. Repeat both sets of exercises 8 to 10 times each.

## SAILOR PULLS

Stand with your legs apart. Stretch up one arm above your head, then the other, alternately, as though you were pulling an imaginary rope. Do 12 repeats.

## CHEST FLING

Stand with feet apart, knees slightly bent. Hunching your shoulders forward, extend your arms out in front of you at shoulder level, backs of the hands facing each other, palms outward.

Swing the arms out and back behind you, chest forward, head back and straightening the legs. Repeat this exercise 8 to 10 times.

## RELAXER

This exercise is similar to the yoga Pose of a Child; do it to relax after the previous exercises.

Kneel on the floor, legs together. Your buttocks should be on your heels and your arms by your sides with your knuckles resting on the floor.

Lower your head to the floor, sliding your hands (palms up) back to lie on each side of your body.

With chest on your knees, turn your head to one side and rest for as long as you like.

## LEG STRETCHES

Kneel on all fours on the floor, resting on your elbows. Stretch your right leg out behind you, bending the knee and lifting the leg as high as you can. Straighten it out behind you and point the toe. Lower back to kneeling position. Change legs. Do this 6 to 10 times with each leg.

# Weights

Selecting the right weight is a matter of testing. If you are a beginner, start with 2 lb (1 kg) weights in each hand and try to do 12 repetitions of an exercise. If this feels too easy, then you need to use a heavier weight. If you cannot complete 12 repetitions, the weights are too heavy. You will find your muscles will adapt to the exercise after a number of sessions (perhaps 5 or 6). So reduce the number of repetitions to 6 to 8 and add more weight for resistance.

When you can complete 8 repetitions with the new weight without problems, you need to add more—perhaps 5 percent more, and so on.

This progression is the secret of successful weight shaping. You need to try and increase your workload as you get progressively stronger. Try to exercise on alternate days, but not more than 3 times a week.

### BARBELL SQUAT

Place the barbell on the floor in front of you, standing with feet about 1 ft (30 cm) apart, toes under the bar. Bend your knees and, keeping the back as flat as possible, grasp the bar (hands about shoulder-width apart, knuckles to the front). Keep your head up. Straighten your legs, pushing up, and bend your elbows, raising the barbell up to your chest.

Replace the weight on the floor, pausing at about knee level, with knees bent and back straight, before completing the action. Repeat 12 times.

### BARBELL CURLS

Stand with feet about 1 ft (30 cm) apart, holding the barbell with knuckles facing backward. Bend your elbows, bringing the bar up to your chest. Lower the weight slowly back to the starting position, then repeat 20 times.

This exercise can also be done with dumbbells. It is good for the pectoral muscles – which hold up the breasts – as well as for the arms.

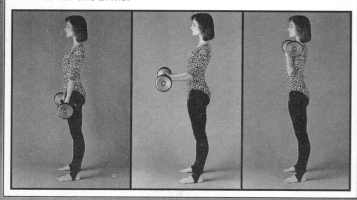

You can do weight shaping with special machines in gymnasiums; with adjustable barbells (a bar with weights at each end), short dumbbells, or even with household equipment such as cans of fruit or vegetables, plastic bottles filled with water, heavy books, socks filled with sand, or bricks wrapped in a towel.

Note: Each time you lift the weights consciously contract your abdominal muscles so that your back is never unsupported.

## STANDING TWISTS
Strengthen your abdominal muscles with this exercise using the bar without weights. (You could substitute a broom handle.) Stand with your feet apart, toes slightly turned out, holding the bar across the back of the shoulders.

Keeping your hips and legs still, twist your body around as far as you can toward the left, then to the right. Repeat 12 times on each side.

## DUMBBELL RAISES
Sit on a chair or seat with your legs apart and a dumbbell in each hand. Keeping your back straight, raise the dumbbells to shoulder height and then straighten the arms alternately, bringing each dumbbell above the head. (This is kinder to your back if you sit down.) Repeat the sequence 12 times.

## SIDE STRETCHES
Stand with your legs apart and a dumbbell in each hand. Bend your left arm across your body and stretch your right arm over your head to the left. Change arms and stretch your left arm over to the right. Repeat 12 times.

## CHEST EXPANDER
Stand with your feet apart, holding the barbell behind you at hip level. Then slowly bend forward from your hips, keeping your back straight. Finally raise your arms up (elbows straight) with head down and back bent. Return to the first position. Repeat 12 times, but do not strain yourself if you find it difficult. Do not attempt this exercise if you have a bad back.

## SEMI-SQUATS
Keeping your back straight, hold the barbell up to your chest, with knuckles facing outward. Bend your knees, just a little. Then straighten up. Repeat 12 times.

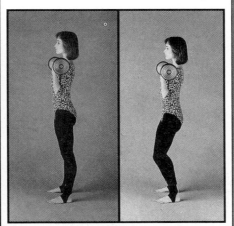

## BEHIND NECK PRESS
Stand with legs slightly apart and the bar of the barbell resting along the back of your neck and shoulders. Raise the barbell above your head. Hold, keeping the elbows straight. Then slowly lower. Repeat 12 times.

## THE PENDULUM
Lie on your back with your legs straight and holding one weight with both hands at thigh level. Keeping your arms straight raise them slowly, lifting the weight up and backward until your arms are stretched behind your head. Return smoothly to the original position. Repeat 12 times.

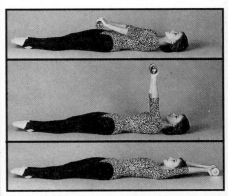

# Aerobics

Aerobics means "with oxygen." It is exercise that builds endurance fitness and is good for your heart and lungs. It is the type of exercise that makes you sweat, and activities with an aerobic effect include jogging, cross-country skiing, swimming, cycling, jumping with a skipping rope, brisk walking and aerobic exercise classes. Disco dancing can be aerobic exercise, so can walking up flights of stairs to your office instead of taking the lift.

When you exercise aerobically, you increase the body's demand for oxygen, so you breathe more quickly and your pulse rate rises. The exertion is making your heart work harder. And, as it is composed of muscle, it becomes stronger with conditioning and pumps more oxygen-carrying blood around the body with fewer heartbeats. An exercised heart is more efficient.

To achieve aerobic fitness, you need to exercise for reasonable periods of time (for example, about 20 minutes) and regularly (about three times a week).

It was an American doctor, Kenneth H. Cooper – considered to be the "father" of aerobics – who determined the effect of exercise on the human body in the 1960s. While studying astronauts and pilots, he evaluated the demands specific exercises make on oxygen uptake and the consequent effect on the heart and lungs.

Aerobic exercise is the application of the principle of overload. You present your body with a challenge to work harder than usual so that the body builds up greater reserve capacity.

Dr. Cooper argues that passive fitness, the simple absence of illness, is a losing battle because without activity the body begins to deteriorate. If you build endurance fitness, you can work without undue fatigue. You have enough energy to do your work and have strength over for leisure activities.

Aerobic capacity is the greatest amount of oxygen you are able to deliver to and take up in the muscles and organs during physical work. For example, a task which previously required a heart rate of 160 beats per minute can be achieved with a rate of 140 if you have built up your endurance with exercise. The effect of exercise training is not so much to improve the heart's performance as to *spare* it by reducing the amount of work it has to perform. But don't attempt to do too much too soon. You need to be fit to do some of the aerobic exercise classes around! Build up your strength gradually, whatever aerobic exercise you choose to do. And do not attempt heavy exertion if you have any heart or back problems, or you are very overweight, without seeing your doctor first.

## Don't forget

● If you want to go jogging or do aerobics classes you need to wear training shoes to cushion your feet and stop jarring. Running shoes need particularly good cushioning and support, so get expert advice before you buy.

● Wear loose, comfortable clothing, such as a tracksuit. For aerobics classes most people wear a stretch leotard and tights.

● Don't workout after a heavy meal. It is best to do vigorous exercise on an empty stomach.

● Don't rush into vigorous exercise without some preparation. Build up fitness slowly and don't attempt too much too soon.

● If you want to workout at home, do the exercises to music. It is much more fun and a better incentive.

● *Always do the warm-ups and cool-downs* to allow your body to return to normal without undue strain. At aerobics classes, you are usually encouraged to lie on your back and take deep breaths as you relax.

● Do not think that you have to push yourself so hard that you hurt. Your muscles might feel stiff afterwards, until you get more supple. Never ignore pain while you are exercising. If you cannot keep up with the rest of an aerobics class, mark time for a bit until you get your strength back.

● Do not strain your back if you are a beginner: exercise carefully.

● Tummy muscles that are out of condition need to be strengthened gradually. Don't overstrain. Once your stomach muscles are toned, your back and posture should improve, too.

● With an aerobics exercise session, the idea is to keep on going, in time to the music, switching from one exercise to the next. But that doesn't mean you are on a treadmill. If you cannot reach the floor, for instance, just go as far down as you can. If you don't feel strong enough for many repetitions, just do a few.

# AEROBIC INTERLUDE

This is continuous, steady, pulse-quickening, and strenuous, so go easy at first. When you are fit you should be able to keep going in time to the music for about 6 to 10 minutes and without stopping and without getting out of breath. If you are not fit, start with a few minutes and build up gradually. When the exercise gets too much for you just mark time with a little walking on the spot until you feel better again. If you feel badly out of breath or have any pains, don't carry on. Know your own limits.

**1** Jog on the spot for about 20 counts, landing on the balls of your feet and then going down on to your heels. You can move your arms naturally in time to the music if you wish.

**3** Jog on the spot, kicking your heels out behind you about 10 times and swinging your arms.

**5** Then, still jogging your knees high in fr Clap hands in front as y alternately.

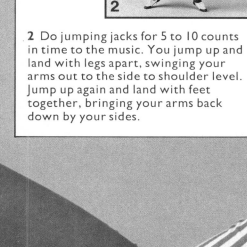

**4** Kick the legs alternately out in front about 10 times, swinging your arms as you do so.

**6** Feet together, make little jumps from side to side, about 10 times.
   Continue exercises 1 to 6 for as long as you want to without feeling breathless or uncomfortable.
**7** To cool down your pulse rate, jog slowly in place for a minute or two, then walk on the spot, breathing regularly.

**2** Do jumping jacks for 5 to 10 counts in time to the music. You jump up and land with legs apart, swinging your arms out to the side to shoulder level. Jump up again and land with feet together, bringing your arms back down by your sides.

...on the spot, lift ...nt, like prancing. ...ou lift knees

## SIDE CURVES

Stand with your feet shoulder-distance apart, tighten and pull in your buttock and stomach muscles, shoulders back but relaxed, arms by your sides.

Stretch your arms above your head and lean over to the right, stretching your waist, but do not bend the top part of your body forward. Think of your body as if it were enclosed between two panes of glass . . . it cannot move forward or backward but stays on the same plane. Count to 8, bouncing gently toward the right.

Return to the upright position, then stretch toward the left. Repeat the exercise on both sides.

## SHOWGIRL BOUNCE

Now put your hands behind your head and bounce gently over to the right for 8 counts, then to the left for 8 counts. Keep your elbows back and don't let your body bend forward.

## FLOOR STRETCHES

Sit on the floor and open your legs as wide as you can – but don't strain.

Keeping your back straight, stretch your left arm up and over your head to the right side, right arm curved in front of you out of the way. Bounce gently sideways for a count of 8. Then straighten up and stretch over to the left.

## TOP TWISTERS

Stand with feet apart, knees slightly bent. Hold your elbows (at shoulder level), and twist the top part of your body to the right. Look over your right shoulder, and bounce 4 times to the right. Repeat to the left.

## SIDE BOUNCES

Stand with feet wide apart, arms at your sides. Stretch your right arm up and over to the left. Curve your left arm in front of you and bounce gently to the left counting to 8, stretching your waist. Try to keep your hips forward. Repeat on the other side.

## KNEE BOUNCES

Still sitting on the floor with legs wide apart, place the palms of your hands on either side of your left knee and stretch down toward it as far as you can without straining your back. Bounce gently over your knee for 8 counts. Then, keeping your body as low as you can to the floor, "walk" your hands around to the other leg, to a count of 4. Repeat the exercise, bouncing over the right knee.

# STOMACH EXERCISES

## TUMMY TONER

Lie on your back with your hands clasped behind your head, tummy pulled in, knees bent and about shoulder-distance apart, feet flat on the floor.

Keeping your elbows pulled back, raise your head and upper body off the floor as high as possible – feeling your abdominal muscles making the effort, not your arms. Lower yourself down again, but not as far as the floor. Do about 8 to 10 lifts.

*Variation:* put one hand behind your head, but use the other hand to stretch through your knees – reaching forward as you lift your head and upper body. Repeat with the other hand.

## ELBOW TOUCHES

Still lying on the floor, with hands behind your head, bend both knees up, raise your legs and cross your feet in the air. Then, raising the top part of your body, touch your left knee with your right elbow, and then your right knee with your left elbow. Repeat 10 times, keeping your legs in the air the whole time.

## BEAR HUG

Lying on your back, hug your knees to your chest. (You'll like this one.) Lie relaxing for a count of 10. Do this after finishing every stomach exercise.

## KNEE HUGS

Next, hug each knee alternately up to the chest 5 times each – keeping your legs off the ground. Then continue, but lift your head and neck off the floor, bringing your knee as close to your face as you can reach.

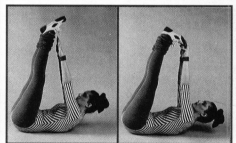

## TOE TOUCH

Lie on your back and bend both knees, then straighten your legs to a vertical position in the air. Try to touch your toes – first when they are pointed and then when they are flexed – raising your head and shoulders off the floor. Afterward, lie down and hug your knees as before to relax.

# LEGS AND HIPS EXERCISES

### VERTICAL LEG LIFTS

Lie on your right side, resting on your right elbow, with palms flat on the floor.

Lift your leg vertically in line with your body, keeping it straight – a scissors effect. Lift it as high as you can then lower it, but to a few inches *above* the other leg – don't rest on it.

Do this 10 times, keeping the toes pointed. Flex the foot and repeat 10 times. Change sides and repeat the exercise with the other leg.

### THIGH STRETCHER

Roll over on to your front, and lift each leg alternately as high as you can. Keep the legs straight and lift and lower each 10 times, with toes pointed. This should *not* cause back pain.

# BOTTOM EXERCISES

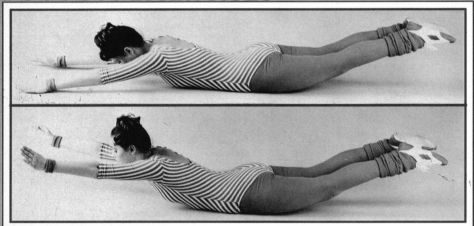

### THE BOAT

Lie on the floor on your stomach, arms stretched out in front of you.

Slowly lift your head and the top of your body and, at the same time, lift your legs as far as you can. Lift your arms off the floor and stretch out. Pinch your buttocks together. Hold, relax, repeat twice. This should *not* cause back pain.

### PUSH OFF

Sit on the floor with your legs out straight, back straight, hands on the floor by your sides.

Bend your right knee, pulling it in toward your body, leaning on your hands. Then straighten your leg and push it out along the floor. Repeat on the other side. Do 10 with each leg (alternately).

### CAT STRETCH

Another yoga exercise. Kneel on all fours, rounding your back like an angry cat, head down. Then bring your left knee in toward your face.

Stretch the left leg out behind you, as straight as you can, head up and arms straight. Raise your leg as high as possible. Return to the first position. Repeat several times. Change legs.

# ARM EXERCISES

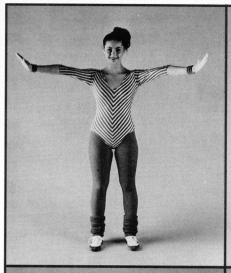

### SHOULDER CIRCLES

Stand up straight, legs together, arms outstretched to the sides at shoulder level, with the insides of the wrists facing down and hands flexed up. Circle each arm forward 8 times, making small circles from the shoulder, and circle backward 8 times. Do not hunch your shoulders. Then make larger circles with each arm again from the shoulder, forward and backward 8 times.

Next, with the wrists downward, point your fingers to the ground and repeat.

Finally, turn your palms upward to face the ceiling and do more circling forward and backward, small and large circles. Keep the arms straight.

### DIAGONAL PULLS

Stand with feet apart, holding your arms straight out in front with wrists together, hands flexed back.

Swing your right arm up and back and your left arm down and back, in a diagonal pull, pulling your chest wider.

Reverse arms for a diagonal pull in the other direction. Each movement should take 2 counts. Repeat about 4 to 6 times.

# Yoga When You're Older

You can start yoga later in life, even if you have not done much exercising before. It is a gentle system and the stretching will help your limbs to stay supple. Older people are inclined to become stiff and immobile, not because of aging so much as from lack of use. Your "aging" symptoms could just be an accumulation of bad habits, whether it is poor posture, shallow breathing, or unhealthy eating. It may take you time to improve, but improve you will. So yoga is very worthwhile.

Join a class if you can — there are many to choose from — where you will get tuition and support. A class gives you incentive to continue, but try these beginner exercises on your own as a taster. Use a mat for the floor exercises and don't be too ambitious to start with. Hold positions for only a short time. Consult your doctor first if you are overweight, or have any history of illness or back problems.

## KNEE PRESS
Simple exercise to try before the classical poses.

Lie on your back on the floor with legs together and arms by your sides, palms down. Bend your right knee, clasp your hands around the knee, and press it to your chest as far as you can. Keep your back straight and press your lower back into the floor. Keep your head down. Hold for 5 to 10 seconds. Then relax. Change legs and repeat.

Repeat with both knees bent together.

## ROCKING
Like the previous exercise, lie on the floor, legs together and arms by your sides. Bend both knees, wrap your

## WARMING UP
Prepare your body for yoga poses with exercises that improve your suppleness. Try to move every part of your body and you will help get rid of stiffness and make yourself more mobile. The exercises marked with an asterisk can be done either sitting or standing. Repeat each set of movements several times but keep them gentle, not too vigorous.

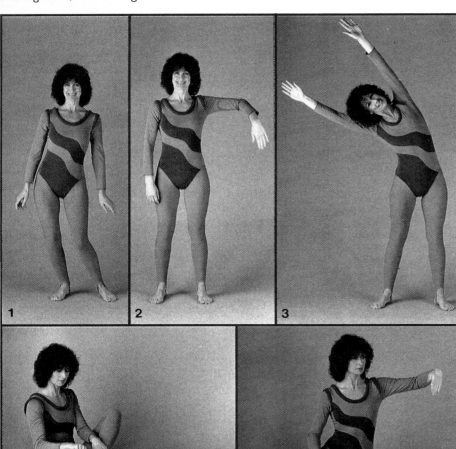

1 Stand with your feet apart, arms by your sides. Exhaling, swing your hips toward the left. Inhaling, swing them back to the center. Repeat to the right side.

2* Circle your left arm (rotating the shoulder joint) first backward, then forward. Then bend your elbow and rotate the elbow joint, circling the lower arm first backward then forward. Repeat with the other arm.

3* Raise your arms above your head. Exhaling, bend over to the left (but try to keep your back straight). Inhale and bring arms and body back to the center. Then repeat, bending toward the right.

4 Sitting down on the floor or on a chair, bend your right leg and place it on the left thigh. Use your hands to rotate the right foot, first in one direction then the other. Change legs and repeat.

5 Lift one arm to shoulder level, elbow bent, and rotate the wrist, first clockwise then anti-clockwise. Wiggle each finger. Repeat with the other arm. Then give both hands a good shake out from the wrist.

hands around them, and press them against your chest.

Bring your head close to your knees and rock gently backward and forward, keeping your back rounded and legs together, gathering momentum. If it is easier for you, clasp hands under the knees. A mat is definitely a good idea for this exercise.

### ARM AND LEG STRETCH

Stand with your feet apart. Join the palms of your hands above your head, with arms straight, back stretched.

Turn your body as far as you can toward the left, swiveling your left foot to point to the left. Now, bend your left knee, keeping the right leg stretched behind you.

Stretch your spine and arms up and look up at your hands. Hold for 5 to 30 seconds, breathing normally. Then relax and repeat with the other leg.

### Variation

After looking up at your hands, turn your head toward the left, and stretch out both your arms sideways at shoulder level. Hold for 5 to 30 seconds, breathing normally. Then repeat, changing legs.

## SPREADING PLOUGH

Lie on your back on the floor, with legs straight, arms by your sides.

Bend both knees in and then straighten them so that your body and legs make an "L" shape.

Pushing down on your hands, raise your buttocks and lower back and bring your legs over your head. With legs straight, try to touch the floor behind you with your toes.

Open the legs, with knees still straight, and spread them as wide apart as possible, toes touching the floor. Try to grasp your ankles with your hands, but don't lift your head. Hold for as long as is comfortable, then slowly uncurl, supporting your back with your hands as you come down.

## SHOULDER STAND

Lie down on the floor on a mat or towel, with legs bent and your arms at your sides, palms down. Bring your knees up toward you and, pushing down on your hands, lift your hips off the floor and bring your legs up and slightly over your head, at an angle of about 45°.

Straighten your legs, using your hands to support your back, pushing it up and lifting your legs higher.

Straighten the spine and legs so you are in a vertical position, still supporting the back with your hands, elbows on the floor. Try to breathe slowly and deeply. Attempt to get your elbows closer together and your hands lower down your back as near the shoulders as you can, keeping your body straight.

Hold the position only for as long as is comfortable.

Come down by lowering your legs to an angle of 45° over the head, then place your hands, palms down, on the floor again and slowly roll out of the position, vertebra by vertebra. When your spine is flat on the floor, slowly lower your legs, bending them as you bring them back over your head.

Note: Don't attempt this exercise if you have high blood pressure or when menstruating.

## SQUAT

Sit on your heels with your arms at your sides and your back straight and stretched upward.

Raise your hips, and taking your weight on your fingertips – hands by your knees – slide your left leg back.

Sit down on your right foot, arms at your sides. Then raise your hips again and drag the left leg back, with knee on the floor, to the starting position. Repeat with alternate legs about 6 times each.

## HALF SPINAL TWIST

Sit on the floor, with your legs straight out in front of you and your back straight. Rest your hands on the floor by your sides.

Bend your left leg up and place it over your right leg, with the foot on the ground close to the right knee.

Twist the body around to the left, bringing your right arm around to the outside of the left knee and holding the right knee with your right hand. Keep the left hand behind you resting on the floor. Look over your left shoulder and twist as much as you can, keeping the back upright. Repeat on the other side.

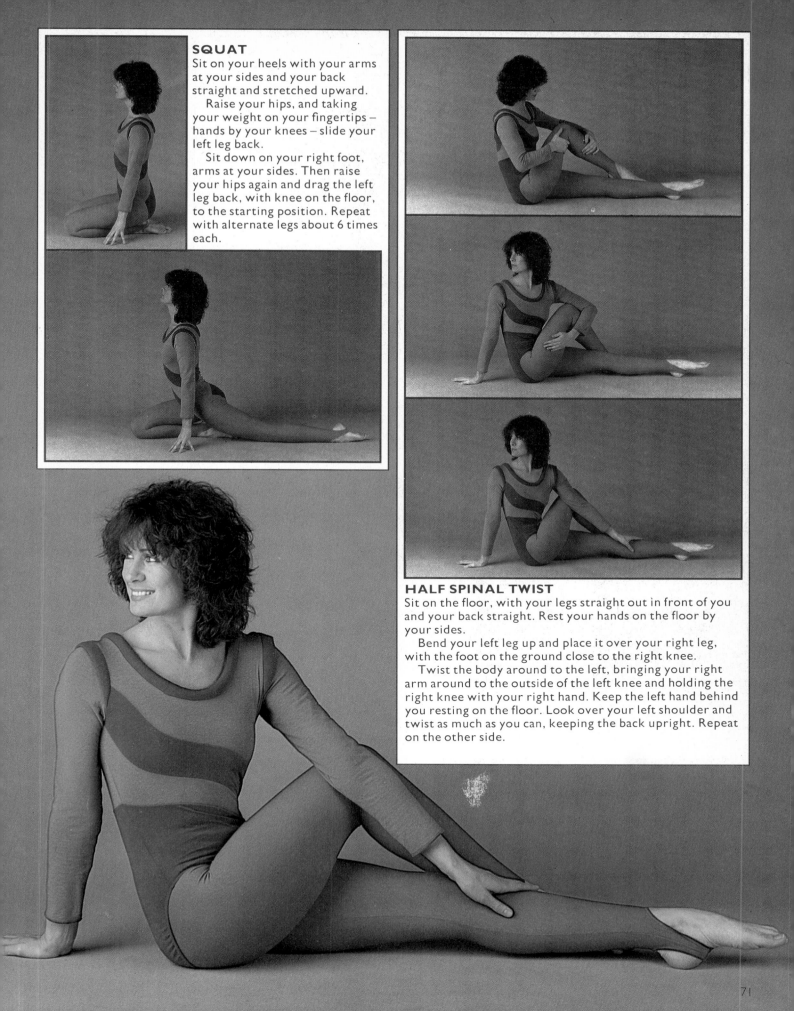

# SPORTS Indoor and Out

If you have often wanted to get out and "*do something,*" then consider taking up a sport. Many are social activities and there is motivation in sharing with others, whether or not in competition.

You will find that one of the more immediate results of taking part in vigorous exercise is renewed energy. Far from exhausting you completely, regular sport devotees find that the motivation makes them feel good, and they feel more awake and prepared to meet challenges. But where to begin?

For a start you could consider jogging, a slow, relaxed kind of running which is a superb aerobic exercise, building stamina and helping to strengthen your heart. You may prefer to jog alone but it can be more enjoyable to jog in a group and it stops you feeling self-conscious at the beginning.

To prevent jarring of the body, you must wear the right kind of running shoes. Running-related injuries can be largely avoided by the correct choice. Factors to consider when buying:

*Cushioning.* The jarring every time your heel strikes the ground is a major stress factor for the body. So the construction of the shoe's midsole is important. The insock with additional pad increases shock absorption.

*Heel support.* Heel stability can be cause for concern. If the heel has too much freedom of movement inside the shoe, your foot can get out of alignment, which can cause a running injury. Good running shoes should have a strong internal heel counter to hold it firm — this is usually extended upward and padded to protect your Achilles tendon.

*Flexibility* of the uppers is important for comfort and to assist push-off.

How to jog sensibly: for a beginner (especially if you are overweight) start by brisk walking. Walk for five minutes, then run for 30 seconds. Walk again until you feel less breathless, then run for 30 seconds. If your pace is such that you can carry on a conversation, you are not pushing yourself too hard.

Walk and run alternately, building up your stamina over a period of time. You may not be able to actually *run* for many weeks.

Aim to do half a mile to begin with, then a mile, three times a week. You can increase your distance as you become stronger.

Here's a consumer look at a selection of other activities to give you a taster.

# Indoor Sports

**Exercise equipment for home use can be expensive. Just what's useful and what isn't?**

### Exercise Bike

A sturdy bike with adjustable pedal power is best — the cheaper ones don't increase resistance, so you have to pedal for longer to get any aerobic effect. Use regularly to exercise the lower body, legs, and abdominal muscles in particular.

Pedal to music if you get bored and try to do a bit more every day.

### Rowing Machine

This gives mild toning of both the upper and lower body and can have a good aerobic effect if you work at it. An expensive investment, like the better exercise bikes, rowing machines have the same kind of fun value: not a lot! But many feel it is worthwhile.

### Skipping Rope

An inexpensive investment and excellent exercise if you do it regularly. The heavy training ropes are better and digital ropes do the counting for you. Fun value:

considerable. Go back to school-days and skip to rhymes or music!

### Free Weights

Dumb-bells and barbells help to tone and strengthen muscles, but as weight-shaping needs to be progressive — you start off with light weights and gradually use heavier ones — it would be best to invest in a flexible set (rather than fixed weights), which you can add to.

Look around before deciding to buy — weights are not cheap. Use homemade weights until you are sure you want to continue.

### Springs

These are 'chest expanders' or

springs joined by two handles which you try to pull apart. Not very suitable for women – most find this type of exerciser boring and difficult. Hand grips and bar benders are not worth considering either, because they provide limited exercise, need quite a lot of strength, and are also boring after a short time.

## Jump for Joy!

One of the best ideas in exercise equipment for home use is the mini-trampoline, or rebounder. Small enough to be used in a bedroom, living-room or office, it can be very effective for all ages. The up-and-down bouncing movement stimu-lates and strengthens the body, and the US National Aeronautics and Space Administration (NASA) dis-covered that for people with similar heart rates and levels of oxygen consumption, jumping on a trampo-line provides a better type of exercise than running.

Bounce to music and this kind of exercise can be a lot of fun. Remove your shoes first, and do a warm-up by flexing the ankles, and beginning a small movement up and down. At first, the soles should not leave the mat. When used to the motion, do an easy vertical bounce rising about three inches above the mat with each bounce.

Then try a slow jog, progress to a faster jog and then a run – this is an excellent aerobic exercise. Other exercises are a good preparation for skiing. The circular rebounders are better than the square shapes because, wherever you land when jumping, the round shape repels you straight up. The rectangular ones have a tendency to throw you from side to side if you miss the center of the mat.

Unlike other forms of exercise, the rebounder affects the *whole* of the body, giving all-over conditioning.

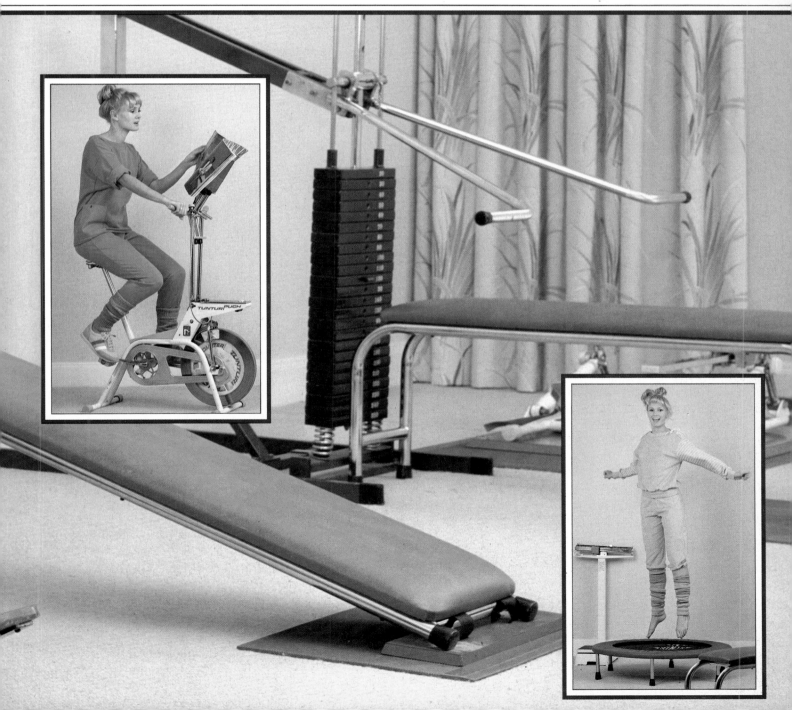

# Outdoor Sports

**Give yourself a tonic, with an activity that gets you out of doors and provides exercise for improving health and well-being.**

### Windsurfing

A rapidly growing sport for all ages, sailboarding has blossomed in the last five or six years, although it was invented as long ago as 1958. It requires some skill, stamina, and strength and you have to like messing about in the water, because you'll be falling in a lot as you learn.

Now declared an official Olympic sport, sailboarding is becoming a popular ingredient of many activity holidays. It's nicer in warm weather, but if you are an enthusiast a wetsuit becomes a necessity so you can go out more often. If you want to feel relaxed and safe, invest in buoyancy aids such as a lifejacket or buoyancy harness.

The sailboard is a small boat which can be fully rigged in a few minutes, and which gives an exhilarating feeling of speed, making you at one with the wind and the water.

You will burn about 200 to 350 calories an hour, and your exertions provide a good workout for the shoulders, arms, upper thigh muscles, and buttocks.

This is a fascinating sport if you are feeling competitive or just want a fun pastime. Two four-hour sessions of instruction should give you a good send-off — you start on dry land.

As sailboarding requires a strong back and shoulders as well as good endurance, build up strength by taking up swimming.

### Swimming

One of the best sports for health, fitness, and all-around exercise, swimming provides excellent cardiovascular benefits (if you swim regularly) and gives fewer muscle pulls than jogging.

It is safer for those who are overweight or out of shape physically, and for older people. Swimming burns up 300 to 700 calories an hour depending on intensity and is particularly good for women because it strengthens the upper body, most women's weakest area, as well as helping to slim the waist.

Try not to swim within two hours of a meal. If you haven't been swimming for some time, start off with a 10-minute session. Try to go through all the strokes to use as many muscles as possible.

Work up to about half-an-hour of fast swimming two or three times a week for optimum benefits.

Drawbacks? You could suffer from swimmer's ear, conjunctivitis, or skin dryness. Both chlorine and salt water are drying to the skin and hair. Take a shower after swimming, then moisturize your still-damp skin. Rinse chlorine out of hair and use a conditioner.

Regular swimmers should try wearing a bathing cap, and goggles to protect the eyes.

## Skiing
It's inaccessible, expensive, and addictive! Yet more and more people are discovering the joys of skiing every year. You learn co-ordination and it is also good for promoting muscle endurance, strength, and flexibility. Cross-country skiing is more demanding than the downhill variety and better aerobic exercise – although carrying skis and sticks around, clad in heavy ski boots, can be testing in itself, especially if you have to do a lot of walking to and from the ski school and ski lifts. If you are a "debutante" or beginner, you will find the exercise value is high because exertion at high altitudes can be taxing.

It is a good idea to try and get yourself stronger *before* you go. Try pre-ski exercise classes and have some lessons on the dry-ski slopes. The better you prepare your body, the more you will enjoy the sport and the quicker you will learn.

## Cycling
Cycling is a very good way to get fit and rates high as exercise – for the heart and lungs and for toning the leg muscles.

If you commute 4 miles (6 km) to work at 12 mph (19 km/h), an average speed, you get the exercise equivalent of nearly 30 minutes of squash or 50 minutes playing tennis. Ride faster – say 16 mph (25 km/h) – and that nearly doubles the equivalents.

Calories expended depend on your speed and how long you keep it up. At 5 mph (8 km/h) you would use about 240 in an hour, at 10 mph (16 km/h) this would rise to about 400 in an hour.

## Roller Skating
A fun way to get fit, good for heart and lungs if you really work at it, and excellent for thigh muscles, this is probably a sport for the young – if only because roller rinks are often aimed at a younger age group.

You can burn up from 250 to 300 calories an hour and the exercise is very exhilarating. Invest in well-made boots and have them properly fitted if you become a fan.

## Tennis

The physical benefits are good — in theory, there's a substantial amount of aerobic activity involved because the leg muscles (largest in the body) are very active and need a great deal of oxygen to fuel them. This means the heart has to work hard. On the other hand, a player can spend a lot of time standing around waiting for a ball. Only skilled players can sustain rallies for long. Concentrate on your game and you can forget your out-of-court worries. Tennis is relaxing, as long as you don't get so competitive that you feel stressed about winning and losing!

You can burn up to 400 calories an hour depending on how hard you work and how many balls you run for. An average sort of game would only use up about 200 or so calories.

Have some training and the game will become even more enjoyable. Perseverance is essential if you want to improve your game and make the most of your exercising.

## Squash

This great all-year game has become a very popular sport these last ten years. Because of the boom, there are now more courts than ever before, but you have to be consistent about booking.

You only play for about 40 minutes at a time, but this can be highly competitive and demanding. For amateurs who run around a lot, squash can be a good exercise for the heart and lungs, and for overall fitness if you play at a fast pace.

However, it is not a good idea to take up squash if you are over forty and have not played any vigorous sport before. The first rule in the squash safety code is to "get fit to play squash, don't play squash to get fit!" If you wish to play squash regularly and competitively when you are older, you need regular medical checkups.

Badminton can be as physically demanding but most middle-aged players play doubles, while squash is played as singles and so harder work.

You can burn up from 300 to 700 calories an hour, depending on the pace.

## Golf

Rather slow to be good exercise, since you only hit the ball from time to time. You can have a good walk, of course, and if your golf course is hilly, carrying your golf clubs up and down can even be aerobic. But that isn't very usual. Still, it's nice to be out in the open air, and this is a social sport. It is competitive though, so not completely relaxing.

# INDEX

**PHOTOGRAPHIC ACKNOWLEDGMENTS**
Kobal Collection: 25 top left and bottom right
Mansell Collection: 25 center
Mary Evans Picture Library: 24 center and bottom, 25 top right
Reproduced by courtesy of the Trustees, The National Gallery, London: 24 top
Courtesy *Successful Slimming* magazine: front cover, 26–7, 34–5, 76–7
Tony Stone Associates: 21 center, 46–7, 76 insets, 78–9
Zefa: 21 left and right

The publishers would like to thank the following for providing clothes and equipment for photography: Marks and Spencer, The Dance Center, The Pineapple Dance Center, The Fitness Center, Arena, Lillywhites.

Diets: Jenny Salmon
Exercise consultant: Wendy Cook
Medical adviser: Dr Alexander Gunn